WIFE SWAP

Based on the Wife Swap programme produced for Channel Four by RDF Media
Special thanks to everyone on the production team who has helped with this project

First published 2003 by Contender Books
A division of the Contender Entertainment Group
48 Margaret Street, London W1W 8SE
www.contendergroup.com/books

This edition published 2003

1 3 5 7 9 10 8 6 4 2

ISBN 1 84357 106 4

With thanks to the following photographers for their kind co-operation:
David Lane, Sian Trenberth, Mark Pinder, Sean Pollock, Quintin Wright, Andrew Hasson
Matt Squire, Richard Ansett, Des Willy, Chris Ridley, Michelle Jones, Simon Buckley.

Production: Sasha Morton
Contributor: Chris Longridge
Design: Button One to One, London
Colour separations: Radstock Reproductions Limited, Midsomer Norton, Somerset
Printed and bound in Great Britain by Butler & Tanner Limited, Frome and London

WIFE SWAP

The Official Book
To Accompany the Hit TV Show

Paul Webb

Contents

Wife Swap from the Top

Wife Swap is one of the most popular reality TV programmes of recent years, giving the viewer the rare opportunity to witness first hand what it is like to experience someone else's life.

It follows a simple format, in which two wives trade their houses, husbands and lifestyles for ten days to see what it's really like to live in another family's home. What is it like to live with a different spouse? How will she cope being a mother to a stranger's children? Will the family like or loathe her? How much conflict will there be over either set of rules? Will either couple learn anything from the experience and will it affect their relationship with each other in the future? For the first five days of the challenge, each wife will fit into their new family's lifestyle, and adopt their daily routine – whatever she thinks of it. For the remaining five, she will have the opportunity to bring her own ideas into the household and her temporary family will have to follow her rules!

Despite the provocative title, the show is not about sex, but about relationships, as Stephen Lambert, programme maker at RDF Media, the production company behind the series, explains. 'It is about people learning about their own relationship through experiencing other people's. Every family unit is its own little civilisation. We all do things differently, yet each of us assumes that the way we organise our lives is 'normal', that it's the obvious, common-sense way to run a household – when in fact to another family it will seem strange or unreasonable or just wrong. Unless you immerse yourself into another way of living,

you'll never have the experience to compare with your own way of doing things. Wife Swap gives people this opportunity.

But *Wife Swap* is not just about dumping people into families with vastly different backgrounds or incomes. It's more about the nuances and real details of ordinary people's lives – who walks the dog, cleans the loo or makes the decisions. The two wives might come from fairly similar backgrounds and seem alike in many ways, but that doesn't automatically mean their lifestyles, relationships or parenting styles will be the same.

The differences between the two households are summarised in the manuals that each wife is required to complete before she leaves home. After five days of living by the rules the new wife finds in her temporary home, the tables are turned and for the remaining five, she is able to run things her way. As Lambert points out, *Wife Swap* is largely a documentary, but it also has elements of a game show as well. Each wife – or contestant – has to endure ten days in a new household, coping with the stresses and strains of a new family. At the end of the swap, a reunion is held, the perfect opportunity for the woman to see their beloved spouses again and to explore any issues that have arisen out of their experience.

It is this format that makes *Wife Swap* such compulsive viewing. Like most great ideas, it is a very simple one that appeals to an ancient and very powerful emotion – that the grass is greener on the other side. At some point in their lives, most people will have fantasised about having a sexy new partner and perfectly behaved kids, or living in a Posh-and-Becks'-style mansion with servants. *Wife Swap* actually gives the swapees the chance to try this alternate life out for real.

As the first two series have shown, the grass can be greener – and life better – in their new homes, and some wives have returned home determined to ring in the changes. However, many of them have the opposite experience, realising that in fact they are incredibly lucky to have the lives and families they do. Even where there have been some post-*Wife Swap* relationship problems, the programme shows that by and large we settle down with people who suit us.

One of the most revealing things to come out of the series is that it only takes a tiny change in the way we are used to doing things to make us feel uncomfortable or upset. You don't have to swap a super-rich family with a low-income one in order to produce the sort of tension that makes really watchable television. Anne and Diane in series one were both quite similar, with comparable houses and families, yet it was the different way they looked at life, and the nature of their marriage in particular, that made the experience so uncomfortable for both of them – especially for Anne, whose time with 'male chauvinist' Graham was clearly not something she would ever want to go through again. Ever!

The series concept was created in early 2002 when RDF Media executives met for a planning session to try and come up with a new programme for Channel 4. After painstaking research and some last-minute refinements, the wife-swapping idea was born and from the outset the concept seemed like a real winner. The couples were then selected and filming began in the summer of 2002, with the first series airing in January 2003. It hit the headlines and was an instant word-of-mouth success. From the very first episode, when the nation was treated to the fireworks between Dee and Lance, and Sonia's battles with Dee's daughter, the shows provoked the kind of reaction the programme makers had longed for – gasps of incredulity and mammoth discussion around the nation's watercoolers as colleagues chuckled, 'Oh, my God! What were they like?'

Wife Swap's success is partly due to the fact that it appeals to everyone, regardless of class or age. Although the show is centred on the wives, it looks at the whole household and everyone participates in the action.

Wife Swap's ratings started high and continued to rocket, as word spread about the addictive series. These are the ratings for the four episodes of series one, which was broadcast on Tuesday's at 9pm. Did you help make up the numbers?

Episode 1: Dee and Sonia 07/01/03   **3.9m viewers** (15.5% audience share)

Episode 2: Michelle and Carol 14/01/03   **5.1m viewers** (20.6% audience share)

Episode 3: Kate and Tracey 21/01/03   **5.6m viewers** (22.4% audience share)

Episode 4: Anne and Diane 28/01/03   **5.5m viewers** (23% audience share)

From the safety of sofas across the country, the viewing nation was able to compare what they saw on their screens with how their family lived their life. Not only did the series prove to people that their own partners were not nearly as bad as they thought they were, it also highlighted to teenagers across the land that their parents weren't the unreasonable bores that they took them to be – at least, not in comparison with the adults they saw on their screens, anyway.

Wife Swap also attracts a wide range of viewers because it's just really great car-crash telly. On the one hand, it's straightforward entertainment in the best fly-on-the-wall tradition. On the other, it generates fascinating conflicts and clashes of personalities, in the same way that chat shows like *Jerry Springer* do. Larger-than-life characters are let loose on each other in a modern, and bloodless version of gladiatorial combat. You don't need to have a degree in psychology to appreciate that each episode is a fascinating exercise, as different character 'types' are put through their paces.

What *Wife Swap* represents is a lesson in how to make *really* good television, and proves that a simple, straightforward idea can become a phenomenon. The series certainly captured the attention of the press and got the viewing public talking. After a few on-air trails on Channel 4, there were a lot of bums on seats waiting to see what this partner-swapping lark was all about, and it's safe to say they weren't disappointed! It was clear that the events of the after-swap reunion, and the subsequent homecomings, turned the conflict into new-found confidence. Self-awareness was very much part of the package, and that made *Wife Swap* a demonstrably positive experience for all the couples who took part, and ultimately satisfied the audience with a happy, but realistic, ending.

The media reaction was immediate: *Wife Swap* was compulsive television, with most commentators expressing a horrified fascination with the personalities from each episode. A number of reviewers thought that the format was designed to encourage conflict and therefore provided the required entertainment factor for the average twenty-first century television viewer. By watching to see just what the couples learned from the experience (admit it, you were thinking 'These people are going to be so embarrassed when they see themselves' too!) we were also learning about our own relationships.

Imagine leaving your life behind to step into someone else's for a while. As this new documentary proves, it could be Heaven… or Hell. This is fascinating TV which proves the grass ain't always greener.
The Sun, 7 January 2003

What the Papers Said
The *Wife Swap* Word on the Street

It's not uncommon for a show to provoke water-cooler conversations the day after transmission, but when the trailers alone are enough to get everyone talking, you know you have a hit on your hands.

RDF Media and Channel 4 couldn't have chosen better participants for their series' opener than Sonia, Dee, Lance and Dave. Expectations were high in the lead-up to the show's debut after Channel 4 showed sneak previews of the couples' rows, and audiences weren't disappointed. The next day, instant catchphrases like 'You're being Hitler – and Hitler died,' and 'I didn't know they made women as useless as that,' were being repeated in workplaces from Carlisle to Canterbury. Lance's perceived chauvinism, or Dave's transformation from doormat to lawmaker became the hot discussion topics of the week. That was just the first episode; over the next month, all anyone had to do to prompt fits of giggles in their colleagues was yelp, "Carol! ...Carol! ...Carol!" à la Barry. And don't even mention his porridge...

The show generated an equally strong reaction in the press – *heat* suggested, tongue in cheek, that as the series coincided with the announcement of the Queen's New Year Honours list, the creators of *Wife Swap*, rather than the usual group of faceless bureaucrats, should be granted knighthoods.

Among the broadsheets, *The Daily Telegraph* and *The Times* were transfixed by the chalk-and-cheese element, while *The Independent* recognised that there was another side to the show beyond the shouting and conflict: 'If you watched with your partner,' wrote their reviewer, 'I suspect you'll have ended up talking about more than what you saw on the screen.' Both aspects made it compelling television – the arguments were fascinating and, needless to say, funny, but what brought viewers back each week was something else. The wailing and gnashing of teeth may have grabbed the headlines but, more significantly, the participants and their audience were invited to confront their own assumptions about the 'best' way to keep a marriage together and raise a family.

Were 'male chauvinist' Graham and his kids right to expect wife Diane to do all the housework? New wife Anne certainly didn't think so, feeling that the disorder of Diane's household led to far too much pressure being placed on her as the housewife. Diane, however, was dismayed in turn at the regimentation of Anne's family, and seemed to prefer being in control. But who was right? This was the key to the series: it posed questions without easy answers, but struck to the core of viewers' own relationships. Men and women at home, able to see the reality of other couples' home lives, not only boggled at the alternative ways of life, but were also forced to wonder if their own relationships were as perfect as they'd like to believe.

Maybe their own partner secretly harboured a desire to change the routines of a lifetime, but were afraid to rock the boat. Perhaps it encouraged them to bring up a few issues of their own. More than anything, *Wife Swap* was about opening the lines of communication. As *The Sun* said, 'This excellent series can make or break a marriage.' But did they mean the participants' or the viewers'?

Aside from the reviews, the show also received massive popular acclaim. The first episode landed 4.7million viewers as Channel 4 cannily scheduled a Sunday late-night repeat, having realised how much of an effect word-of-mouth would have over the following days. In subsequent weeks, the figure rose to 5.7million. For the record, only *Big Brother* has managed to top that figure for the channel in recent years. It's rare to come across a show that manages to be jaw-droppingly entertaining, quotable and thought-provoking in equal measure. 'Must-see' is an over-used term in broadcasting hype, but for once, *Wife Swap* was a series that truly deserved the accolade.

'We had this idea...'

Hilary Bell is the Commissioning Editor for Channel 4 and she was responsible for giving the *Wife Swap* concept the 'green-light'. Here's what she had to say about the show and how it came about...

Stephen Lambert and his wife, and my partner and I were at a dinner party and we observed another couple there. In that gossipy way that you chat, Stephen and I were wondering who really wore the trousers in that relationship? We were saying how difficult it is to work out what really goes on in someone else's home, shut away behind four walls from the rest of the world and that the secrets of a relationship would be very hard to put across on television, because what is really telling, and interesting, about a relationship is the domestic minutiae that go into it.

At my next ideas meeting with RDF Media, Stephen came up with the concept of a programme about just this and he called it *Wife Swap*. We both felt that this would be great television territory, that it was a really good idea, and I already had a lot of confidence in Stephen after working with him on *Faking It*. Fortunately I'm in the position at Channel 4 where I can say 'Yes, go with it', and I did! We were after the little things in a home that made up a relationship, not in wife swapping in a sexual way – that would be just another grim documentary about 'swingers', whereas what we wanted was something much more interesting and unusual.

We decided to get the directors who would work on the programmes in for meetings and to try to sit down to work out the details. Six weeks later they presented their ideas, and had come up with Household Manuals.

Most of the structure for what became the eventual programmes was there, but they weren't at all sure how to end each episode. I suggested that we get the couples to meet each other face to face at the end of their swap. So we finally arrived at the structure, after about three hours over coffee, some very good biscuits, and plenty of cigarette breaks for my benefit.

You don't get celestial choirs bursting into song when you come up with a great idea like *Wife Swap* turned out to be, you just have a feeling, a sense that 'this could be fun'. I realised, when I went to

RDF and looked at some audition tapes, that this would be a successful series, though there were some problems – like matching a couple to Dee and David Jackson. We didn't know they had any particular views on the race of the couple they may swap with until the morning the filming began; that wasn't why we matched them with Sonia and Lance. It was just that the director had reached the stage where she needed to find someone to swap them with.

I assumed the show would work, because of the confidence I had in RDF and our earlier discussions, but it wasn't until Stephen asked me over to watch the 65 minute cut of that episode that I realised we had a hit. It was one of those 'Oh my God' moments as we walked out of the room; I told him it was brilliant. On the other hand I was still quite nervous about how it would be received. I was convinced that this was really compelling television, and I realised other people thought the same when a tape of that first episode, which I gave to my assistant, got borrowed and shown round by people in the office at Channel 4. The tape became a hot property, with people talking about it a lot, saying

'Have you seen this?' That was exactly the word-of-mouth response that it eventually got from the general public.

The next two films were also very good, and I commissioned a fourth to go with them.

I'm really pleased with the second series, and the episode with the two brothers (Jason and Dave) is very moving. It's about a man afraid to be a father.

One of the joys of the format is that it shows people who, unless they are put under a type of stress, having their values put under pressure, aren't really very self-reflective. So the experience lets them reflect, lets them look at their lives and make changes, which is a very positive thing.

The one thing that isn't positive is that there's no sense of sisterhood, and I find it very depressing how judgmental of each other the women are. The response to the episode with the working mother was also very strong and rather worrying. Alright, she was a rather extreme example, commuting two hours each way to go to work, but it was still the case that many people took an incredibly hard line against working women.

I think the great strength of the series is that it presents you with extraordinary characters, who if they were fictional you'd have said were too over-the-top to be believable.

As a series it's been a great success, so much so that our researchers found that it belonged to that small group of events where people lie about it, saying they'd seen it when they hadn't, because they didn't want to feel left out of a powerful experience that a lot of people had shared and enjoyed.

It also demonstrates the richness of attitudes and approaches to living that we have in this country. I hadn't expected how seriously people would take the challenge to their value systems of having someone else come into their family, experience them and then comment on them. It shows how most of us don't have a real opportunity to step back and look at ourselves, that we take our way of life for granted, that we slip into certain habits of doing things, a way of living, and the experience of those taking part in *Wife Swap* has been very positive, in that it has given them that chance to look at and change their lives.

The filming of each episode took place after extensive research into the potential candidates, many of whom were attracted to the programme by an nationwide advertising campaign. Ad's were placed in the local press and people were asked to contact Channel 4 if they wished to take part, but the whole process was far more pro-active than just putting flyers into newspapers. Community groups were contacted, while supermarkets and other family-friendly places were extensively leafleted.

Posters advertising the series, inviting people to find out more about taking part, were left at shops near council estates, nurseries and swimming pools – locations which helped the production teams track down the 'right' sort of family.

FAMILIES WANTED

Channel Four is making a documentary series about modern family life.

Ever wondered how other couples cope with hectic lives, split chores, childcare, spend money and have fun?

Ever thought what it would be like to step into someone else's shoes to see how they run their household?

Would you be interested in a family challenge??

**If you are interested and would like more information
Please call or email ASAP**

Dee and Dave found out about the programme at their local supermarket, while Sonia, who was the manager of a gym, became interested when her workplace was contacted by a researcher looking for suitable candidates.

Persuading families to take part was easier when referring to it as a 'family challenge' rather than suggesting a 'partner swap'. The words 'wife swap' weren't used at all, in case the potential sexual connotations put some people off – or encouraged the wrong types to come forward! The fact that *Wife Swap* wasn't about throwing keys into a bowl and jumping into bed with a complete stranger was something the media frequently commented on... occasionally with a slightly disappointed tone. In fact, viewers were more likely to find dirty clothes on display, rather than no clothes at all!

Another important aspect of the show that the researchers were keen to emphasise was that the swapee might not end up anywhere more exciting or luxurious than their own humble family home.

Candidates could well end up swapping with their next-door neighbour or someone of a similar background. What they would get from the swap was the chance to help another family and bring back some really positive ideas to their own lives. Even so, plenty of households were ready to take the plunge, but there was a lot more 'real life' in the other people's lives than some of the contributors could have possibly anticipated!

Once a family had come forward, they were visited by researchers who filmed them so that the team back at RDF Media could assess whether or not the couples were suitable. Given that families were involved, it wasn't simply good enough to find a fabulous wife or husband – the *couple* had to be interesting. It was no good just having one person who would make a great television character, if their other half was as dull as ditch water, or the relationship between the two wasn't going to create sparks on screen.

When a family had been chosen, it was important that the researchers could find another family who would be compatible with them. The directors of the episodes had to have a good idea about the sort of couple they were looking for. Did they want to film a mixed-raced marriage? Or find a household where the couple shared everything, or where one partner did none of the housework at all? The possibilities were endless. Once a couple had been booked up, the search was on to find an interesting match. With any couple, the most important factor in determining the swap was what went on within the household, in terms of family relationships, rather than differences of race, religion or income.

When researching suitable couples, a questionnaire was sent to them, which allowed directors to get the necessary basic information about each family, and so enabled them to make their shortlists. Here's one we made earlier, for you to tackle yourself…

Swaps
Phone Call Sheet

How did you hear about the programme?

How long have you and your partner been together?

Are you married?

Tell us about your relationship.

What do you have clashes/conflicts about?

Do you both have defined roles?

Children and their ages? Tell us about them.

Do you or your partner work?

How would you describe your personality and that of your partners?

Is there room for improvement in your relationship?

Who wears the trousers in the relationship?

Describe your home. Is it a sociable house?

How do you split the chores?

How do you split the childcare?

How would you describe your parenting style?

How do you discipline your children? (views on spanking etc).

What are your views on spending? Do they differ from your partner's?

Do your views on men's and women's roles differ?

What are your interests outside of home and work?

What interests you about this swapping concept?

What would you have in your household manual for the visiting wife?

What do you hope you and your partner would learn from a swap?

Having actually come up with a suitable swap, it was vital for the research team to check that no one involved had a criminal record and that there was no alcohol or substance abuse in the family. The couples were also screened to check that they were psychologically suitable to undergo the stress of the *Wife Swap* experience.

During the filming of each show, the director stayed with one of the households, while the assistant producer was attached to the other one. Shooting took place throughout the day, so each two-person team (director plus assistant, assistant producer plus assistant) were with the wife from early morning until last thing at night. Surprisingly the contributors soon became used to having a camera and sound crew trailing them around, and it became entirely normal to have their every action caught on film.

What is amazing about *Wife Swap* is that the people involved in the melodrama unfolding on the screen aren't actors, but members of the general public, living out their lives and discussing their most intimate thoughts in front of a camera. When the crew and the other people in the house weren't around in the room, the wives or husbands retreated to the 'privacy' of their bedrooms, and completed a video diary.

These direct chats to camera provided some of the most illuminating moments of each episode. The camera as confessional is hardly a new concept, but in some cases it helped the viewers feel more sympathetic to the people involved, after seeing them express their most intimate feelings about the swap.

With every episode of *Wife Swap*, the relationship between the director and the families was crucial to the success of the film. Thus stressful situations were able to be defused, and walk-outs prevented.

Although the best laid plans do go awry and sometimes the production teams couldn't stop things coming to a premature halt, they at least ensured that the end was as painless as possible, and the couples got together for the reunion.

During the time of the swap, starting from when the women were preparing to leave their own homes, many hours of film were shot. A lot of the footage was fairly repetitive, ie; ten shots of the wife getting up, making breakfast or moaning about what she had to do. But this was necessary as no one knew what a day would produce. Would today be the day when tempers flared and tears were shed? By the end of the swap, both wives tended to have had enough, and were simply getting through the day. Either they were barely on speaking terms with their temporary 'husband' and desperate to get back to their real one, or they had bonded successfully and learnt some lessons, so were keen to get home where they could put any new ideas about their relationship to work.

Editing each episode took a few weeks. It was a slow and painstaking task to sift through literally every minute of footage in search of a good television moment. Making a finished programme involved more than just finding some juicy rows or movingly tearful moments, as editor Mike Gamson explains:

'The episode has to work as a whole. You have to decide, out of the many different lines you could go down, which basic plot, and which sub-plots, you are going to show in the course of the programme. But you have to develop the plot lines in a coherent way, and you also have to maintain a balance between the two households – which isn't always easy – while still getting the maximum amount of good television from the hour's material. Quite often one household will be more interesting, more dramatic, than the other one, but you can't just focus on one family rather than another. You have to find something to watch from the second home, and in a way that contrasts with or comments on what is going on in the more exciting household.'

It is the opportunity to enter into other people's lives and their innermost thoughts from the comfort of our own homes – which are, of course, perfect – that makes *Wife Swap* such compelling viewing. But you could you do it yourself? Over the next few pages, you can find out if you've got what it takes to be a *Wife Swap* star!

Make Your Own *Wife Swap*

Want to be a swapper? Here's what you're getting into!

1. One or two days are needed to film set-ups with both families, highlighting each daily routine, including work, childcare and social activities, backed up by interviews outlining their family values. The household manuals can be completed at this point, or in the research period.

2. On the day of the swap, the wives pack up and say goodbye to their families. A pack is given to each wife containing keys and directions to their new home.

3. The wives arrive at their new home and look around the place and read the Household Manual before meeting their new husband and family.

4. The wives live the first five days of the swap according to the Household Manual they inherit. Depending on the distance between households, the wives will either continue their normal job or take on the job of the other wife (within reason).

5. The wives call a 'Change of Rules' meeting on their fifth day to tell their new families how they will be running the house for the final five days.

6. The wives live the final five days of the swap according to their own rules.

7. On the tenth day the couples meet up to compare and contrast their reactions and experiences.

Your cut-out-and-keep Production Schedule

Still fancy the idea of making your own *Wife Swap*?
Follow our handy tips...

1. Allow a couple of months to find another couple who are insane enough to want to swap lives with you. Don't be shy about asking, just expect to be laughed at/verbally abused or given the come-on. Have a sharp retort ready to slap down the latter type of comment.

2. You'll need two weeks of filming to generate an hour of film for impressing the family with at subsequent Christmas parties. It's well worth booking a week off work afterwards, to recover from trying to make a good impression and not swearing on camera. This is when you can let your hair down and catch up on your sleep. After all, you'll have been getting up at 4am to get your make-up on...

3. It'll take about six weeks to work out how to get all shaky camcorder footage off the recording gizmo and on to a 60-minute tape. This is the point when the sleepless nights kick in and you realise you forgot to warn your parents that you smoke. They're about to find out all your dirty little habits now. You have been warned!

Production Staffing

Don't forget, it's not just you and your long-suffering partner who are in this. You'll need to give suitably snappy titles to the crew (otherwise known as your friends and neighbours).

Executive Producer — Will stop filming you when all that cleaning and ironing footage gets boring.

Production Manager — Keeps an eye on the budget. It is the Production Manager's responsibility to ensure the housekeeping money isn't all spent on beer and Pringles.

Runner — Should pop to the shops for batteries, tapes, KitKats, etc. on demand.

Production Coordinator — Skivvy to the crew at large. Should ensure there's plenty of fags available and that the best crystal doesn't get broken.

2 Producers/Directors — May need to be brought down to earth when they are reminded they aren't making *Schindler's List*. There is no earthly reason for them to be hanging upside-down in a stairwell getting art-house shots.

2 Assistant Producers — Will be found holding the ankles of Producer when they are getting that crucial art-house shot...

Central Castings
Helpful Hints

1. Both husband and wife must be relatively intelligent but most importantly must have self-insight. They have to be able to tell the viewer what they are feeling, but not be too far along *The Road Less Travelled*. Too much navel gazing doesn't make good viewing. (Geri Halliwell types, take note.)

2. You must be capable of completing the challenge, physically and mentally. If your partner is generally incapable of organising an orgy in a brothel, they aren't going to be very helpful once you've left and they've got to make some organisational decisions of their own. No shrinking violets need apply.

3. It is paramount that all involved are not scared of confrontation and have the ability to debate intelligently. It doesn't matter how loud you can shout, the verbal dexterity of a stand-up comedian tackling a heckler is more the standard you are looking for.

4. The first day of the swap is very important and will form the majority of part one. Drain every last bean out of this – once it's over, it's over.

5. It's really important that your contributors feel that there is no respite from filming (apart from work situations or places where the husband and wife are apart). If they get a whiff that there will be time for them to talk when the cameras have gone, they will do so. They will anyway, but at least let them think there won't be time.

6. Check the contributors' video diaries daily, both to make sure they are doing it and also because it will give you more of an insight into how they are feeling. Start your own diary to remind yourself what you looked like before filming. After a few days of this, you'll be booked into The Priory for a full personality reconstruction…

Quite possibly the most important document you'll ever write. Don't forget, honesty **is** the best policy!

1: Household Chores

How often do you clean your home?

Who does the cleaning in general?

Is this done voluntarily, or only when asked?

Who does the following, and how often...

- Hoovering?

- Dusting?

- Tidying?

- Ironing?

- Cleaning the bathroom?

- Clothes washing?

- Cleaning the kitchen?

- Washing up?

- Loading the dishwasher (if applicable)?

- Cleaning the car? Gardening?

- DIY?

- Decorating?

- Other / what?

2: Cooking/Meals

How often do you sit down and eat together?

Where do you eat?

When are meal times?

Who prepares breakfast / lunch / dinner?

Does your partner help?

Who cooks and when?

What are your top three dinners?

Do you all like eating similar sorts of food?

Do you have any special dietary requirements?
Is there anything you won't eat?

3: Shopping (Food/Household Goods)

Who does the shopping for food and household goods?

Does your partner help?

How often do you go food / household goods shopping? When do you go?

Where do you usually shop?

Write a shopping list for the first week.

4: Shopping (Clothes)

Who shops for clothes?

Where do you go?

How often?

5: Daily Routine

Morning:

What time do you usually get up?

How much time do you need to get you and your family ready in the morning?

Do you ever get a lie-in?

What time do the kids need to be at school?

How do the kids get to school? Who takes them there?

Daytime:

What time do the kids finish school?

How do they get home?

Do they have any extra classes / activities after school? If so, when and what?

After school, do the kids generally come home / have friends round / go round to friends?

Evening:

What time do you get home from work?

Do you help the kids with their homework?

Do the kids have to be in / in bed by a certain time?

How do you spend your evenings from Monday to Friday?

What time do you go to bed?

6: Weekends

What do you generally do on Friday night?

What do you do at the weekend?

- Saturday daytime?

- Saturday evening?

- Sunday daytime?

- Sunday evening?

7: Social Life / Leisure

When you go out, do you tend to go out as a couple, or individually?

What kinds of things do you like doing when you go out as a family / as a couple / as individuals?

8: Kids

Who does the childcare? What does it involve?

Do you like to have a routine with bedtimes etc. for the children?

How do you discipline the kids?

Do you spend time without the children?

What things do you and your partner disagree on with regard to childcare?

9: Family

When do you see your family / in-laws?

Do you go round to visit them? Do they come and visit / stay with you?

Do your relatives help look after your kids?

10: Friends

Who do each of you call in times of trouble?

How often do you see them / speak to them?

How often do friends come round?

11: Work

What hours do you work in the office / at home?

Do you bring work home in the evenings?

12: Finances

What is your average combined income after tax?

How much do you each earn?

Who controls the money?

How much do you each contribute to the household funds?

Are you spenders or savers?

How much do you spend on food & household items per week?

How much do you spend on bills per week?

How much do you spend on clothes per week?

How much do you spend on going out per week?

How much pocket money do the children receive per week? Are there conditions?

How much money do you save / invest per week?

*How much do you each spend on treats / vices
per week?*

List any extra costs in a typical week.

13: Relationships

Who has the final say in family decisions?

What tips can you give for coping with your other half?

How do you like to be treated?

What happens when you disagree on something?

14: House Philosophy

Sum up the philosophy of your house and life within it.

Final Reminder

If you lie when you complete this, you **will**
get found out!

Here comes the science...

You don't have to be barmy to want to take part in the series, but it helps. Dr Glenn Wilson, co-author of *Fame: The Psychology of Stardom*, gives us the low-down on why people do it.

What do you think about the concept behind *Wife Swap* – taking two women and swapping their lives for ten days?

It clearly makes good television, and I think it can be helpful for the people involved, given that it takes them out of the cocoon of their own environment and enables them to discover how other people live. It has the potential to shake people out of any sense of complacency about their relationships, and might also be able to identify where a relationship has gone wrong. It can help put things right, or give someone the impetus to move away from a relationship that is now wrong for them. Either way, it's a learning experience.

What about the risks of someone having their life exposed on television?

Life is all about risks! There's no shortage of takers for the various forms of reality television. As reality TV goes, *Wife Swap* is quite low on the list for potential embarrassment or humiliation – certainly when you look at the Japanese endurance programmes which are little short of torture for the public's amusement.

What does *Wife Swap* tell us about the nature of fame?

It shows how fame has changed in recent years. What makes you famous nowadays is appearing on television. There's no need for an actual achievement, like winning a Nobel Prize, or having done some heroic deed. Exposure in the tabloids or on television now generates fame, not the other way around, and people become celebrities if they appear often enough in the public eye. With reality television, people become instant celebrities simply because they have appeared on the box, not because of any inherent talent.

Reality TV is immensely popular. Why do you think this is?

Many people yearn to be part of a community. It can be argued that human beings are ideally suited to belong to groups of, say, 150 people, including family, neighbours and work colleagues. Modern society can seem far too large to form a cohesive group or can, alternatively, be very isolating if people don't live in a community where personal interaction is the norm. Television communities – like Albert Square or Coronation Street, for example – become an alternative, and give a sense of belonging.

With a programme like *Wife Swap* we become, in a sense, members of the most basic community – the family. *Wife Swap* lets us share the temporary wife's experience, but from the comfort and safety of our sofa. We don't actually have to deal with the situations they find themselves in, but we can enjoy watching them.

Is there another appeal to reality television?

Yes. In *Wife Swap*, for example, the people you see on screen are quite normal, in that they aren't super-rich or talented or unusually attractive in the way that some actors, models or celebrities are. The viewer can identify with them and the dilemmas they face on the swap: it could just as easily be them up there on the screen.

What are the potential downsides to taking part in such a programme and becoming a media personality?

Your fame is entirely dependent on appearing on a television programme rather than on having a talent or skill, however interesting a person you may be. However, once the programme is over, that celebrity status can quickly fade away and there's the risk that you can be left feeling very deflated and empty, or with a strong sense of anti-climax.

What about the risk to relationships?

A relationship that goes on the rocks as a result of a programme like *Wife Swap* is one that will probably have had major cracks in it anyway. No one would want to see a relationship break up because it made good television, but as the point of the programme is to give people space to look at their own lives from a very different context, it might well be that realising that a relationship needs to change, or end, can be a very good thing. As it happens, the experience of most partners in Wife Swap seems to be a positive one, so taking part in the programme obviously had a happy ending.

Could the *Wife Swap* experience make the contributors feel unsatisfied?

The impetus behind *Wife Swap* – the desire to see whether we want to change our lives – is a very natural one. We have more choices and freedoms today than our grandparents ever had. The downside to this is that we worry we aren't getting enough out of life and that other people's children are better behaved, their homes are nicer, and their partners are more affectionate. A reality television show like *Wife Swap* is a chance to see for ourselves, whether as viewer or, more dramatically, as one of the people taking part, if that is true.

WIFE SWAP

Series 1 Episode 1

WIFE SWAP

The Couples

Dave and Dee Jackson have been married for 18 years and have two teenage daughters, Carol and Mary. Dave describes himself and his wife as 'large people' who take little exercise and whose diet consists of ready-prepared meals, apart from on Sunday's, when Dee shows off her culinary skills and prepares 'a full Sunday roastie'. They live in a crowded flat, where, according to a proud Dee, they have over 2,000 cuddly toys. Dave does most of the housework while Carol volunteers that Dee just 'sits on her backside and watches television'.

Sonia Dyges and Lance Francis have known each other for two years, but have only lived together for the last five months. Sonia has two children, Kimberley and Luke. Both partners are health conscious, and Sonia exercises regularly at a gym while Lance takes an obvious pride in his appearance. Their flat is modern and minimalist. Lance holds traditional views and is a firm believer that it's a man's role to provide for the family, and the woman's to look after the home.

Name: **Dave Jackson**
Age: **46**
Occupation: **Bus Driver**

Arriving

On arriving at their homes for the next ten days, both women are given the opportunity to have a snoop around. For the first five days, they will live under the rules of the household they are to stay with: for the second, they will introduce rules of their own choosing, which the resident family will be required to stick to religiously.

Initially, both woman make straight for the kitchen and check out the fridge. Dee is given a hint of what may lie ahead when she spots that none of the food is pre-prepared and there are some suspicious-looking contents – a packet of coconut milk, for example – that she and her family would never eat. After spending some time poring over the household manual, she is further bemused by the family's love of curried goat, something that makes her conclude, 'They aren't English!' By contrast, Sonia is amused to see the Jacksons' fridge is almost devoid of fresh food, chuckling, 'Not much in the way of actual food in there!' Someone's going to go hungry then.

Reading through her household manual, Sonia seems to be getting the better deal when it comes to feeding the hungry hordes, realising that she doesn't have to cook for the family on a daily basis: 'We eat frozen microwave meals except on Sunday…Well, that's handy… I like the sound of that!' On reading that Lance and the children expect their meals to be cooked from scratch, Dee's eyebrows shoot up in horror, 'I haven't done that for years!' she gasps.

Meet The Family

Both sets of introductions seem to go smoothly enough, but first impressions are always important. In private, Lance comments that Dee is no sex symbol and definitely not his kind of woman, but he admits that isn't why she's there, so just hopes that she will fit in well with the family.

Alone in her room and speaking to her video diary, Dee confesses that Dave will be utterly horrified to find that Sonia is black. However, on seeing Dave and Sonia's initial meeting, Dee's insistence that her

Name: Lance Francis
Age: 38
Occupation: Bakery/Restaurant Business

husband will be completely thrown by having a black woman in the house seems vastly wide of the mark. In fact, from the outset, Dave and Sonia seem to hit it off and get along like a house on fire. The Jackson girls stay very much in the background – Mary quietly radiates a brewing hostility towards their new houseguest. Dave tells Sonia he is surprised to find that she is 'a dark lady' and fishes around to see if Lance is too, offering up Dee's disapproval of mixed marriages, 'At the end of the day, why do you have to mix it?' he muses. Sonia predicts possible fireworks between Lance and Dee – watch this space.

Getting To Know You...

After the initial period of politeness while settling in, the gulf between the two families' way of life soon becomes clear and tensions begin to surface. In both households this brings out long-standing issues, which are not helped by the presence of a stranger in the home. At Sonia's house, Dee and Lance soon realise that they don't approve

of, or like each other too much. To straight-talking Dee, Lance seems arrogant and insensitive, expecting her to do far too much housework, and making no allowances for her being 'up and out of the house for work by 7am and not back until gone seven in the evening'. She thinks he is far too strict and OTT with the punishments he hands out to Sonia's children. She is also particularly irritated at his smoking big fat spliffs around the house.

£50 a week on weed – that is a drug!

It isn't just that he smokes weed that gives her the hump, but that he does it in the flat, in front of her and the children and correctly forecasts, 'We're not going to see eye to eye.' Give that woman a gold star! Never one to lose a battle, Dee is determined to deal with the dope issue when she gets her turn to set the household rules. Meanwhile, she and Lance clash on the amount – and type – of cleaning that she should do. Pointing to a sink full of dirty crockery, Lance snipes that he had been tempted to clean it himself, but as

Do your children have mouths like sewers? How can you stop the kids 'effing and jeffing'?

Dee is supposedly there to take on all Sonia's duties, shouldn't she get a move on and clean it up herself? Dee looks on with faint interest from her chair. Talking of cleaning, hasn't she ever learnt how to use a mop, asks Lance, grumbling

She doesn't actually mop the floor

Over at Dee's place, Sonia and Dave are becoming firm friends. Obviously horrified at his lack of parental authority and at the way the girls swear, not just in front of, but at their dad, she feels very much on his side when it comes to his dealing with his daughters. She tells him,

I think they love you very much, but they don't respect you.

Dave seems to welcome a bit of adult female support with the girls' unreasonable behaviour, giving the impression that Dee doesn't intervene much when their daughters get out of hand.

Lance, by contrast, has very fixed ideas about the children doing what they are told: 'I may dress like this, and I enjoy going clubbing, but in some ways I'm quite traditional, and I have very strong views about how people should behave.' He's not wrong there. When, in the course of the first five days, Lance 'grounds' both children, insisting they stay at home until their mother returns, Dee is convinced that he has over-reacted to something that could have been dealt with more diplomatically, considering a firm word and a warning would have been more appropriate. Firm words are also on the agenda between her and Lance, and she confides to her video diary that if he wants war then boy, is he going to get it.

Dee's reaction to Lance's approach to discipline reflects her more laid-back attitude to discipline at home, and is probably also influenced by the fact that, as Dave puts it, 'she wears the trousers'. Seeing the man of the household lay down the law is an unusual experience for her and the grounding incident only reinforces her already hostile view of how Lance behaves. Oh, dear... tears before bedtime!

Who does the cooking and cleaning – which are sources of friction between Lance and Dee – aren't even issues at the Jackson household, given that Sonia has so little to do, but worsening relationships and behaviour issues are major problems that she must tackle. Carol was initially as lippy to her father as her sister Mary, but has quickly mellowed under Sonia's calming influence. While Carol likes her 'new mum' and clearly wants to be liked in return, Mary, the older of the two at eighteen, takes the opposite approach. Initially, both girls have mouths like sewers and 'eff and jeff' whenever asked by their father to do something they don't want to. Although Carol soon begins to behave more maturely, Mary's language simply gets stronger – and louder! She and Sonia are clearly heading for a major confrontation… but who will win this battle of wills?

Turning The Tables…

The first five days have established that Dee and Lance don't get on, and Lance certainly isn't a man to beat around the bush, delivering succinct retorts such as,

*That's why you are so fat –
because you sit on your arse all day.*

Do grown-ups and cuddly toys go together? Perhaps your home could benefit from a good de-clutter...

Meanwhile, Dave and Sonia are ticking along very nicely thank you, despite the fact that Mary detests Sonia's presence and now resents her sister for treating Sonia as a refreshing new role model. But it's when the women get to impose their own rules that the fireworks really start.

The macho Lance, who believes that men should run the house and enforce discipline, is told by Dee that she is lifting his grounding of the children. Despite an attempt to argue, Lance reluctantly gives in but is clearly furious at the news. Then Dee hands down the harshest rule: a complete ban on smoking weed, on the grounds that it is bad for the children's health and for hers. Passive smoking of tobacco is bad enough, but she certainly isn't going to put up with inhaling his pungent fumes any longer. The fact that he is being criticised by a woman, to his face, and in front of the children, does not make him a happy bunny.

At the Jacksons' home, Sonia's changes are even more radical. She plans to take the whole family with her to the gym for a punishing workout. Always the diplomat, Sonia's criticism is always calm and diluted with a compliment, so 'fat' isn't mentioned, but 'fitness' is.

A second rule is also established – the girls are to do whatever David asks, without answering back or turning the air blue. Now hang on here, Sonia! On a roll, she decides to give all the rooms in the flat a revamp though they can of course return everything to its normal state once she has gone. The tidy-up is going to happen, whether they like it or not.

The makeover is surprisingly drastic. The living room looks twice the size after most of the clutter is shifted, and in a shock move, Mary's bedroom is stripped of its huge quota of cuddly toys. As Sonia has said on first seeing the room, it looks more like a six-year-old's than a teenager's, but you can't help feeling sorry for Mary when Sonia takes down her pop star posters as well!

As Sonia predicts, Mary 'has a baby' when she sees what has been done to her room, but instead of shouting back, Sonia just turns to Dave (who has agreed to back her up, whatever she does) and asks him what he is going to do about it. Looking a little stunned, the 'new' Dave springs into action and follows Mary into her bedroom, demanding she apologise to Sonia immediately. A little shocked by hearing her father raise his voice possibly for the first time since her birth, Mary stomps back into the living room, shouting 'Sorry!' at Sonia at the top of her voice in a tone that makes it abundantly clear she is anything but, then strops back into her bedroom. It's just one step too far for Dave and the nation holds its breath as he finally snaps. From behind the closed bedroom door, the normally mild-mannered man shouts back angrily – 'You did what? You said what?' – which is maybe why Mary changes her mind and offers a slightly more sincere apology to Sonia. Although clearly appalled at Mary's behaviour, Sonia remains calm throughout the heated exchange. Amazingly, given she's just been personally insulted, she is able to rationalise the young girl's earlier outburst and is incredibly tolerant.

Determined to hit a more positive note, Sonia digs out their trainers and takes the family down to the gym, where Carol and Dave get into the spirit of the visit and actually do a workout. Dave confesses that the last physical exercise he had was in a P.E. class in 1971, stunning his personal trainer into a bewildered silence. Mary, however, refuses to take part and watches her family from the sidelines whilst clutching her boyfriend whom she has taken along for moral support.

Mary also draws the line at a night out at a black cabaret evening, so a smartly dressed Dave and Carol accompany Sonia to the gig. The combination of a stylish outfit, a new hairdo and Sonia's frequent reassurance that far from looking fat she looks 'really glamourous' boosts Carol's confidence no end and she looks genuinely pretty as she gets ready for her night on the tiles. The collective sound of a nation letting out an 'ahhh' of approval is heard up and down the land…

No fun-filled evening has been arranged by Dee however. Her clash with Lance over her new rules has provoked Sonia's daughter into having a row with him, too. Kimberly, taking Dee's side, tells him that he is an arrogant man who refuses to listen to anyone else. The fact that Lance isn't her father makes the dispute even more bitter, with Kimberly insisting that Lance will never be a part of the family, while Lance taunts that he is, and that she'll have to get used to it. At this rate, surely Sonia is going to wonder if it would be worth staying at Dave's house instead! Totally fed up and frustrated by Lance's taunts, Dee lets him know what she really thinks of him, uttering the immortal line,

You're like Hitler – and Hitler died!

For much of her stay, Dee appears to be taking things easy, sitting in 'her' chair in the living room, reading *The Sun* and staring into space. However the peace is soon shattered when Lance, who is supposed to follow her rules for the second half of the swap, refuses to accept her ban on dope smoking. According to him she is simply 'ignorant' about the issue, declaring,

You have been brought up to believe crap.

Fireworks explode once again when Lance attacks Dee's weight and her choice of menu. Lance doesn't like the sort of packaged food that Dee is serving up, arguing that it's unhealthy and inedible. The gloves come off when he brings up her size,

I can prove your food's crap — look at you!

This line of attack hits a nerve with Dee, who shouts back twice as loud. She refuses to accept that she has a problem: she is '100 per cent fit', having recently had a medical check up proving just that – clearly Lance doesn't know what he is talking about. Both assume that the other's criticism – of weight and diet on the one hand, of marijuana smoking on the other – are cultural differences made worse by personal animosity. Lance and Dee both accuse each other of talking 'crap', and the bust up gets progressively more personal and heated. Dee tells Lance how it is:

You're the most ignorant piece of shit in shoes I've ever met

while Lance curls his top lip in disdain and says,

I didn't realise they made women as useless as that.

Remember that a few kind gestures can go a long way and to paraphrase Sir Elton John, 'Sorry' needn't be the hardest word.

Blimey. By the time the swap is due to end, Sonia has firmly established her authority in the Jackson household, but the same can't be said for Dee. After a series of arguments, they do seem to have cleared the air a bit. In fact, Lance compliments her on standing up for herself and says that she has come across as more of a human being. Dee, flummoxed by having received a compliment from him, simply says, 'Yes, I am a human being', and they both allow themselves a tiny smile. Could this be the start of a beautiful friendship?

With the long-awaited reunion looming on the horizon, Sonia comments on how much she is looking forward to seeing Lance again: 'I appreciate Lance more now because I feel that he is the sort of person I need... someone strong,' while Lance, in a rare emotional moment says touchingly, 'I need to have my lady back...'

Taking Stock

Reunited in a local restaurant, it is clear that it is the Jacksons – and Dave in particular – who have been most changed by the swap. Dee is immediately put on the defensive by his determination to put into practice the lessons that he has learned from the experience: that the girls need to be brought under control, telling her 'You give in to them too much' and that he needs Dee to back him up if this is to be achieved. Clearly upset, Dee rounds on him, telling him things certainly will be different as she is going to throw him out! It's Dave's turn to be caught off guard, but he carries it off well, 'If you want to throw 18 years down the swannee, that's up to you,' he says calmly. Lance and Sonia spend most of the reunion listening to the Jacksons argue. When Sonia points out how much better behaved, and open to change, Carol is than Mary, Dee reacts strongly, saying that everyone prefers her younger daughter and Mary is therefore isolated and needs more understanding. The accusation has hit a nerve. Although Dee blurts out, 'Piss off!' as soon as Sonia makes the comment, she also reaches for a handkerchief. It seems Sonia's criticism of Mary has produced tears, something that the bitter rows with Lance never provoked.

Whatever Dee's public defence of her daughters and her lifestyle, it becomes clear, when she gets home, that Dee has clearly thought about her own experience over the last ten days. On returning to the flat, Mary gives Dee a cuddle, but Carol refuses. Could Carol have turned against her mother? Mary sarcastically says, 'Excuse me, she does cuddles with Sonia!' and Dee gets even more upset, retorting 'Oh, have I got to paint myself black? I'll go and get some boot polish', while Dave looks on, unamused.

For a moment it looks as if Dee has learned nothing: or perhaps she is genuinely hurt, to have her daughter behave in such a reserved fashion after her absence. That things have changed, and that Dee has absorbed some lessons, is soon made clear, however. When Mary complains about what Sonia has done to the flat in her mother's absence and says she wants it back to normal straight away, Dee stands firm, telling her daughter she hasn't had a chance to experience the new look yet, which she wants to give a try for a couple of weeks. She also isn't taking any flak from the kids any more, and when Mary answers back, she threatens to ground her, '"Grounded" is a word that's going to be coming into this house!'

Sonia's homecoming is predictably more peaceful and Lance is indeed relieved to have his lady back. It seems that of the two families, it is Dave and Dee's that has been most fundamentally challenged, but will the *Wife Swap* update reveal the real truth?

The View From The Sofa

Given that *Wife Swap* is about putting women in very different home environments to those they are used to, the choice of couples was very perceptive. The episode highlighted that more than any racial differences, there was an obvious gulf between the two couples in terms of relationships: both between the adults and between the adults and the children. The question of taste also came into the equation. Lance's response to Dee's breezy mention of her home containing 2,000 cuddly toys was an incredulous 'Say what?' while Dee found his flat 'rather plain'.

So, who *really* wears the trousers in your home?

Sonia was surprised to hear that Mary was 18 years old, thinking she looked 'much younger' but the real issue was behaviour rather than looks: she acted like a child rather than a young adult. One reason why Sonia chose to 'clean up' the flat was that she thought Dave and Dee allowed Mary and Carol to live as if they were little girls. Removing the childish toys and clutter and turning the room into 'something more like a teenager's bedroom' might help them move on and behave more like teenagers than children.

Given that the relationship between children and parents was so central, there were some aspects of family life that remained mysterious, such as what time did the children go to bed? Did Dee and Lance, Sonia and Dave, chill out together in front of the television of an evening, as they would have done with their real-life partners, or did they head straight for their own rooms after a family meal in the evening?

What was clear was that Lance ran a traditional household where his woman did the chores, while at the Jacksons Dave was the housekeeper, as well as holding down a job. Sonia's children were kept on a very short leash and the resentment this caused blew up after Dee challenged Lance's way of doing things, while Dave and Dee's handling of their daughters was exactly the opposite, with both girls swearing at their parents as a matter of course.

Dave's lack of support from Dee was brought home to him by Sonia not just backing him up, but having identified that there was a problem in the first place. Of all the people involved, the swap seemed to have the strongest effect on Dave, who was determined to stand up for himself. And although her initial reaction had been very negative, it was clear from the way she acted on her return that Dee's stay in a family where the children were noticeably well-behaved had a profound effect on her, even if she hadn't wanted to say so in front of Lance, either during her stay or at the reunion afterwards.

While Dave and Sonia came across really positively in this episode, Dave had clearly 'seen the light of day' in the course of the swap, and was determined to make changes to the way his family operated: his temporary wife had been the person who had shown him the errors of his ways. Sonia had a warm and capable attitude, which gave her a confidence and a calm that enabled her to shrug off any problems. But it was her constant good humour even in the face of a screaming fit, that came across most strongly. She sympathised and sided with Dave who she liked, but made it clear that in her own life she wanted a man who was tougher than he was.

This first episode launched *Wife Swap* which soon became a word-of-mouth success, capturing the nation's imagination with its entertaining cast and proving to be unmissable TV.

Household Manual

Sonia, Lance, Kimberley and Luke

1: The Relationship

Lance has the final say in family decisions.

If anyone is moaning the best thing to do is to ignore them and go into another room. When we have an argument it can last for hours. We should all be treated with respect.

2: House Philosophy

We like to be spontaneous. We like a laid back atmosphere at home. We treat each other with respect.

3: Household Chores

The house is cleaned every day. Most of the household chores are done by Sonia. Lance will not wash up but does clean the toilet. Lance does the DIY and decorating.

4: Meals

We like to cook our meals from scratch using fresh ingredients. Lance does most of the cooking. Our typical dinners are curried goat with rice and peas, roast chicken or corned beef and rice. On Sunday we sit down and eat as a family at the table.

5: Food and Household Goods Shopping

Sonia and Lance shop separately for food at the supermarket and at Brixton market. A typical shopping list for the week would be:

- Rice
- Goat
- Chicken
- Beef
- Lamb chops
- Milk
- Butter
- Flour
- Sugar
- Mixed veg
- Spinach
- Cabbage
- Kallo
- Spices
- Cakes
- Bread

6: Clothes Shopping

We all like shopping for clothes and we go all over south London.

7: Routine During the Week

There is no set routine in our home during the week. We like to do things spontaneously. Lance helps out with the family business on occasions and Sonia spends her time setting up a new dating agency. Luke has lots of after school activities. The children's friends often come around after school.

We spend our weekday evenings spontaneously. We go to bed late at night.

8: Weekends

On Friday night we like to leave the children with a relative and go out on the town. We will do some cleaning on Saturday and we like to chill out at home all day and night on Sunday.

9: Social Life

We enjoy spending time without the children just as a couple. We keep our social life lively and interesting. We like to go visiting friends and relatives.

Household Manual

Dee, David, Mary and Carol

1: The Relationship

We share the decision making. Dee wears the trousers in our relationship.

The best tactic for coping with Dave if he is in a bad mood is to sit him down and ignore him. The best way to handle Dee if she's in a bad mood is to listen and be understanding and loving.

2: House Philosophy

Routine is very important in our home. Cleanliness is of the utmost importance.

3: Household Chores

We share the household chores between husband and wife. We clean our home and do the laundry daily. Washing up is done after each meal and nothing is left overnight.

4: Meals

We eat ready frozen microwave meals, except on Sundays when we eat a roast dinner. Our typical dinners are a roast, bangers and mash, and hotpot – all cooked in the microwave.

5: Food and Household Goods Shopping

We do the food and household goods shopping together at the supermarket, usually on a Friday night. To treat ourselves, we have a meal afterwards at the supermarket. A typical shopping list for the week would be:

- 2 loaves of bread
- 24 packets of crisps
- 6 assorted juices
- pasta
- tin of mushrooms
- tins of spaghetti hoops

- 1lb of ham
- 2 packets of butter
- assorted fruit
- cheese
- 4 tins of baked beans
- 16 boxed microwave meals

- 2 packets of sugar
- 1 box of cream cakes
- 8 rolls of kitchen wipes
- 3 bottles of disinfectant
- 1 bottle of washing up liquid
- 1 toilet rim flush
- 1 packet of tea bags
- 3 packets of chocolate biscuits
- 9 rolls of toilet paper
- 2 boxes of antiseptic wipes
- 1 bottle of bleach
- 4 underarm spray

6: Clothes Shopping

We buy clothes in any shop and Dee does the choosing. We keep our spending on clothes to a minimum.

7: Routine During the Week

Dee works 9-5 regular hours, and David works shifts. The children don't have any activities after school. The children come straight home after school and no friends come round.

We spend our evenings watching the TV from Monday to Friday, and also having a natter together.

Dee goes to bed at 10.30pm and Dave turns in whenever.

8: Weekends

On Friday night we do the food shopping at the supermarket and treat ourselves to a meal in the supermarket eatery. On Saturday and Sunday we go out with the children. On Sunday evening the ironing is done and we get our work uniforms ready.

9: Social Life

We spend all our time together as a family of four. We would rather spend our time with our children than as a couple and we never go out individually.

Ladies… how lazy is your partner?

1. His idea of housework is…

a) getting up at the crack of dawn to make you a cup of tea before running the Hoover round the house.

b) taking equal turns to cook, clean and wash up.

c) watching you do it.

2. He thinks the best way to get a decent dinner is to…

a) cook it himself with fresh ingredients.

b) microwave something tasty in a packet.

c) complain repeatedly about how long it's taking you to cook it, then moan about how bad it is once it's ready.

3. His attitude to work is…

a) up early for a full day's graft, and, if times are tight, a second job in the evenings.

b) an honest day's work for a honest day's wage.

c) "I'm a professional gambler. My job is relaxing and enjoying myself. It's a full-time job."

4. What sort of exercise does he get?

a) A daily five-mile run, three trips to the gym every week and a game of football with the kids on Saturday.

b) He cycles to work and you all go for long walks at the weekend.

c) He last exercised in his school P.E. class in 1971.

KEY

Mostly A's: He seems to enjoy making work for himself. Are you sure you're exploiting this as well as you could?

Mostly B's: While you may occasionally wish he'd get down the gym, remember that then you'd have no excuse to avoid it yourself.

Mostly C's: Well, it's your life, I guess.

Series 1 Episode 2

WIFE SWAP

The Couples

Barry and Michelle Seabourne have been together for 15 years, and married for the last two. They share their house with Stephen, Michelle's son by a previous relationship. Barry has never had a job and is a professional gambler. Michelle is a 'doer', working 60 hours a week as well as doing all the housework. Michelle is an incurable romantic and is looking forward to living with someone with more consideration than Barry, to try 'normal' life for ten days. She's also very open to discussing some of Barry's domestic habits,

Barry's never made me one cup of tea in fifteen years!

Carol and Peter Godby have been married for 25 years and have two teenage daughters, Toni and Leanne. They run a casting agency and Carol also runs a children's theatre workshop. She hopes that the experience will be an adventure and will give her plenty of material for her drama workshops. A workaholic, she lives life to the full and isn't interested in housework, that's Peter's area:

I let him do everything. I'm quite happy.

Name: Peter Godby
Age: 45
Occupation: Runs business in partnership with Carol

Arriving

On arriving at the council estate where Barry and Michelle live, the first thing Carol notices is the large number of Union Jacks – 'Gosh, they're all mad on the Queen round here. They're so patriotic.' Once inside the Seabournes' home, she's greeted by their poodle and a pile of dog mess on the carpet, and wails

Oh, no, I haven't got to shovel poo up, have I?

Michelle, spotting a picture of Carol on the wall at the Godby house, immediately cries, 'Wowee, this is the woman, is it? I don't think she'll like our house'. She thinks the Godbys' house is 'dead smart' and looks forward to making herself at home.

Both women consult the Household Manuals that each has left as a guide to running their home. It becomes immediately clear that the

Name: **Carol Godby**
Age: **45**   Status: **Married**
Occupation: **Runs drama workshop/casting agency**
Location: **Whitfield**
Children: **Leanne (19), Toni (15)**

households are polar opposites when it comes to the allocation of domestic chores. In the Seabourne house, Michelle looks after all the duties in the day-to-day running of the home, while in the Godby home, Peter seems responsible for just about everything. Michelle is delighted that the Godbys' eat take-away's five times a week. With so little cooking to do, she can't believe her luck.

Meet The Family

Both sets of children are the first to greet the temporary new wife. Stephen is quietly friendly, while Toni and Leanne make Michelle immediately welcome with a big hug. Michelle soon gets to meet her stand-in husband, Peter, who explains they have a happy household and that he is a very laid back person: explaining 'I don't go in for conflicts'. Carol finally meets Barry, following her introduction to Michelle's mother, Elaine. She's already wary about meeting the 'Master of the House' after reading Michelle's comments about him in the Household Manual and admits she is very nervous. Even after

Name: **Barry Seabourne**
Age: **43**
Occupation: **Professional Gambler**

giving Michelle's mum a discreet grilling over whether he has any good points, his mother-in-law employs the kind of 'spin' that would have made Alistair Campbell proud and dodges the issue by repeating 'She loves him' in answer to any questions.

Getting To Know You...

Now pay attention boys, Barry's giving out confidential information and you could learn something here... 'You have to be very nice to a girl when you first meet, you give them a special offer. Nothing's no problem... you give them anything they want'. Right. But then, the rules change: be on guard ladies, because once you're settled it's an entirely different ball game. Problems will really only arise if you don't accept that the initial treatment was just a 'special offer' as part of the courtship ritual. It all becomes crystal clear...

Barry gives Carol a version of his special treatment by being nice and undemanding in the kitchen on her first night. Carol is surprised and pleased by her new hubby's behaviour; 'I don't think he's going to be that bad'. Wait and see, Carol, who knows what lies ahead once Barry's special offer expires!

Name: Michelle Seabourne
Age: **35**   Status: **Married**
Occupation: **Works in betting shop**
Location: **Heywood**
Children: **Stephen (15)**

Michelle, by contrast, is taken to the pub, where Peter is amazed to hear her say 'I'm not allowed in pubs' on the grounds that it's bad for her health and, more to the point, keeps her away from the housework. Michelle seems to be enjoying her new found sense of freedom, though she is disconcerted by the lack of things to do around the house. As she explains, both to Peter and to her mother (who has phoned her up to check she's OK), she isn't used to not having to get up at the crack of dawn, let alone – as Peter suggests to her – relaxing in front of the telly. It's just all a bit too decadent for hardworking Michelle.

Carol finds, on waking up, that Barry's 'special offer' has indeed evaporated with the dawn, and we hear him shouting 'Carol!' in a bemused but insistent fashion; it's morning and he wants his porridge. Carol, who is more concerned with how she looks for her day at work, doesn't like his attitude at all:

I find him very, very aggressive. He's a very aggressive man…

Barry, who claims to be 'quicker than the Ferrari team' when it comes to getting out of bed, expects the woman of the house to be equally as speedy at making his breakfast, and he lets Carol know that he thinks she's falling down in that department.

We're not on a fashion parade... all I want is breakfast!

Speaking of fast cars, fitness-fanatic Barry also expects to be driven to the gym, where he can work out of a morning:

My job is relaxation and enjoying myself, that is what I class a full-time job. That is me... the gymnasium, race courses, er, dog tracks...

In between bouts of working in the kitchen, Carol strikes up a good relationship with Stephen, who agrees to join her drama classes, something Barry approves of, 'He loves it. Carol's very good with children. She could bring the goodness out of him.' Carol clearly

Housework versus career. Can you really do it all? In fact, should you even have to?

likes Stephen but tells her video diary that she can't stand Barry: 'He is a really, really rude man who needs to get up off his backside and get a job.'

Once home from another hard day's work, Carol decides to cook Barry a homemade cheese and onion pie for his tea. Not skilled in the kitchen, its preparation takes longer than anticipated and from the comfort of his armchair, Barry is rapidly losing patience with Michelle's stand-in. He suspects that she's deliberately taking her time, in an attempt to get her own back at him for his ungentlemanly behaviour towards her. She wasn't best pleased when he accused her of being lazy because she didn't cook at home, justifying herself with the comment, 'I'm a career woman. The time off that I do have is very much a quality time.' You tell him, Carol. She may be irritated with Barry, but his griping doesn't in any sense challenge her view of her life, her work and her relationships. The cheese and onion pie is eventually served several hours later, but the chef refuses to be riled by Barry's refrain of:

Carol, Carol!

For Michelle, however, the more relaxed attitude to mealtimes is just another of the life-changing experiences she is discovering in the Godby household. Finding herself with an unexpectedly large amount of time on her hands, she broods about her relationship with Barry and about how little time she usually has for herself. Peter explains to Michelle why they have take-away food so often. 'You know when you've been at it all day… you need a reward, because otherwise what's the point? This is our reward.' Can Michelle relax enough to enjoy herself while she's thinking about how different her life could be if she followed the Godbys' example?

Although the wives are not supposed to contact their other halves, Michelle speaks to Barry on the phone, who tells her that he misses her. The fact that she's very pleased to hear this suggests that she isn't used to such compliments. Barry tells Michelle what most women want to hear – that the ship is sinking without her and it's every man for himself: 'Well, I don't do f*** all when you're not here, all operations stop, don't they? Carol's come in but obviously she's not like you, is she? You're just a one-off, aren't you? You're what you call wonder-f***ing woman.' Ah, bless… he's such a sweetie.

He is far less forward with the compliments to Carol the next morning, especially when she challenges him about his attitude towards her. A succinct verbal encounter ensues:

'I find you a bully.'
'Right…'
'Unreasonable.'
'Right…'
'Loud.'
'Right…'
'And quite a difficult man and I think I've tolerated a lot from you.'

Barry eventually agrees that the way he behaves may be partly due to his competitive relationship with Michelle, which keeps him on a heightened level of aggression the whole time. Or is it just because he's quite happy to leave Michelle at the helm and enjoy his first-class passenger lifestyle?

Their relationship is put to the test when Barry and Michelle are allowed to meet for an evening to celebrate their third wedding

Has he told you lately that he loves you? 'Don't ask, don't get' or should those three little words always be spontaneous?

anniversary. The romantic rendezvous takes place in a car on a windswept moor, but almost immediately Mrs Seabourne announces that there will be some changes to their relationship once she returns. The time apart has given her the opportunity to see what her life could be like, but far from conceding anything, Barry immediately goes on the offensive, claiming that it's Michelle who's made him the way he is. Michelle can't believe what she's hearing, retorting 'Don't be blaming me for what you are'. It's not looking good for our 'Professional Person of Leisure' but he pulls the meeting back from the brink of disaster when, during the prolonged row, Barry lets slip the three magic words: 'I love you, right, but I don't show love in the way that 90 per cent of the population do'. Michelle is over the moon as it is the first time in their stormy 15 year relationship that she has actually heard these words. Don't… I'm filling up.

It's at this point that the action-packed swap comes to end, so we sadly don't get to see Carol laying down the law, or Michelle applying her 'operation' to Peter's household. Still, the reunion could prove interesting!

Taking Stock

It's time for the couples' reunion and surprisingly Michelle seems to have had a massive change of heart. After feeling hard done by in her usual role with Barry, she now claims that her life isn't actually that bad after all, announcing to the Godbys, 'I'd rather have my life than yours'. Peter looks on unconvinced while five million viewers collectively pick up their jaws from the floor.

Michelle admits that she has missed the daily drudgery of looking after her man – the endless washing, ironing and general housework. Mischievously, Carol declares that she thought Barry had been nicer to her than he normally was with Michelle, citing his mother-in-law as a witness to his new behaviour. Michelle is astonished to hear that on one occasion her husband made Carol a cup of coffee. It kicks off the kind of heated debate that Becks and Fergie would've been proud of as the two argue whether or not it really is the case that Barry has never once made his wife a brew. In fact, Carol's suggestion that Barry proved to be relatively adaptable is something of an insult to Michelle, suggesting as it does that if he really wanted to, he could be more flexible with her, too.

Then it's handbags at dawn as the two women get deep down and personal. Michelle makes a point of criticising Carol's ability as a housewife: 'You didn't do any housework... You couldn't fit into my house because you don't take orders or instructions from anybody.' Carol replies with a quip about polishing Michelle's halo, while Michelle retorts,

You've failed at being a housewife and I think for a woman to fail at being a housewife is absolutely ridiculous.

Ooh, it's just like the sexual revolution never happened!

Back at home, both wives sum up what the experience has meant for them. Michelle says 'It's made me think that the way me and Barry are is actually important, that we have actually got love and that the grass ain't greener on the other side, definitely not.' Carol finds the experience an affirmation of her satisfaction with her existing way of life, and is grateful for having done the swap, as she explains; 'What I've got out of this experience is a realisation that everybody doesn't live the same. You know that but you don't realise it and perhaps everybody's not as fortunate as I am, so it's made me aware of what I've got.'

The View From The Sofa

This episode featured a collection of very strong characters, with Carol displaying a real strength under fire, especially when subjected to the onslaught of her name being called on a seemingly never-ending basis. She seemed tough and capable, and though she was annoyed with Barry, there was no sense of her wilting and cracking. The emphasis of this show, however, was far more on Michelle and Barry's relationship and it would have been fun to see the usual changing of rules halfway through the programme.

There was no conflict between Peter and Michelle, because there was nothing to spark a row: Peter acted as he normally did around the home, which left nothing for Michelle to do. He came across as a nice guy, but it seemed that Michelle liked to see a bit more testosterone in her partner. Barry, the archetypal Northern chauvinist, became an instant celebrity, revered for his unabashed attitude to male/female roles within his house. The fact that he also earned a living by going to the races elevated him to hero status in some circles and it's safe to say the job title 'Professional Person of Leisure' is one that many men and women would like to add to their CV!

Porridge. Is it really the way to a man's heart?

There were no clashes between the wives and the children of the households that they went to live in. On the contrary, Carol persuaded Stephen to go to drama classes, and he carried on with these after the swap finished. Given that he had come across as such a quiet boy, this was an achievement on his part and a positive outcome to the swap.

If one word could be used to sum up this episode, it was romance. At one point Michelle said, 'I've got a lot of love for Barry. I'm probably romantic where Barry's not. Love to Barry doesn't mean a thing'. There was no doubt at all that Michelle loved Barry, and Barry presumably loved her back, but wasn't keen to say so. Viewing the episode from the sofa, you couldn't help feeling that Barry slipped in the bit about loving Michelle at a timely point in the conversation. Until that point he had been on the defensive, and it looked as though the relationship – which is obviously a very comfortable one for him, despite the rows – was on the verge of collapse as a result of Michelle's time away.

Those three words completely changed the whole meeting, and she was overjoyed. His nonchalant acceptance of her desire to kiss, allowing her the opportunity to throw caution to the wind with, 'On the cheek, yeah' was the calm magnanimity of a victor, someone who with a brilliant tactical stroke has snatched victory from the jaws of defeat, against all the odds. Just goes to show that all that betting had sharpened his skills at judging when to make the right call.

While male viewers may have admired his debating skills, and manipulative dexterity, female ones will have empathised with Michelle, and understood her pleasure in hearing her husband's declaration of love. Many were also probably wondering why she'd stood by her man for so many years without hearing these words before. Their's came across as the kind of relationship that Country and Western songs are made of! It was clear that Barry's declaration made an enormous impact on Michelle and made her earlier comment about her husband not being a romantic seem like the understatement of the century.

Their relationship raised, in a fairly extreme form, the question of how much romance a couple might reasonably expect. The programme didn't address the same issue with Peter and Carol, though it would have been interesting to compare them on this level. They were clearly a happy couple with a calm, established routine: but was there any romance in it? Can you have a happy marriage without romance? Was Michelle being rather clingy when she demanded frequent reassurance about how much she was missed, or needed, or was that the natural reaction of someone away from a home where she was never actually praised or thanked for all that she did? So many questions, so little time…

Is it important to look your best first thing in the morning? In our poll, 90 per cent of women said 'abso-bloody-lutely', while the other 10 per cent were still getting their beauty sleep.

What the Papers Said

Last week's edition (Dee and Sonia) had such spectacular catfights, that tonight's wives-take-over-each-other's-families programme can't possibly match it. Mind you, it has a decent try – mainly thanks to Barry, an aggressive, lazy husband who expects to be waited on hand and foot. His real wife, Michelle, says "Barry never does anything. Never made me a cup of tea in 15 years." No wonder her instructions to incoming wife Carol are: "Do what you're told... keep the master happy. Do everything!"

Evening Standard, 14 January, 2003

THE WIFE SWAP QUIZ, PART 2

How good a cook are you?

1. You're running short on fresh lemon for a particular dish. Do you...

a) quickly nip round to the shops before they close to stock up?

b) adapt the recipe to suit what you have?

c) fish a manky old bit of lemon out of the bin and hope no one notices?

2. Your man has come home from work hungry. Do you...

a) already have dinner waiting on the table?

b) quickly knock something tasty together for him?

c) take three and a half hours to incinerate a cheese and onion pie?

3. A domestic routine for you means...

a) carefully planned meals based on availability of produce, and a cleaning rota.

b) regular meals for all the family and a Sunday roast every week.

c) take-away's every single day, regular as clockwork.

4. What have you got in your fridge?

a) Fresh meat, fish and vegetables.

b) Some week-old cheese, a bottle of milk, a yoghurt and some celery going a bit brown.

c) Beer.

KEY

Mostly A's: Ooh, hark at Nigella!

Mostly B's: Here's a tip: Worcester sauce hides a multitude of sins.

Mostly C's: It's frankly a miracle that you're still alive to read this.

WIFE SWAP

The Couples

Mark and Tracey Bennett have been married for five years and have a young daughter, Lottie. Tracey is a legal secretary in a large law firm in Manchester – a job that entails a long commute each day. Tracey is proud of her job, 'I'm an individual. I've built up my career over twenty years'. Mark works in a local factory, so he can pick Lottie up from the nursery. They are firm believers in family treats when they are able to spend time with their daughter and are happy with having just one child as Tracey doesn't think she'd have enough love for another.

Trevor and Kate Thomas have been married for 10 years. They have five children and a foster child. They don't see their lives, or their raising of children, as being about money. Trevor is a demanding partner, but he pulls his weight, too: he works in a family support unit, is a bouncer at night and is also studying to qualify as a social worker. They are very proud of their children, though they describe them in different terms: when Trevor calls them 'crafty', Kate corrects him, 'No, they're intelligent,' she points out. 'We're passionate about our children,' she says, adding, 'But wouldn't you be about mine?'

Name: **Mark Bennett**
Age: **41**
Occupation: **Factory Worker**

Arriving

On their way to each other's house they naturally wonder about what they'll find when they get there. Tracey has a fantasy about arriving at a mansion with staff – possibly including a butler – so she won't have to work very hard. Uh, oh. When she arrives at the Thomas' house and realises there are six children to cope with she thinks someone's surely playing a joke on her. Tears roll down her cheeks as the enormity of the task sinks in and she sobs, 'I don't think I can do it'.

Kate, who has worried that 'the children might love this new lady and won't want me back', finds that she has arrived at a smaller household than her own with only one child to look after. Kate is worried how Tracey will cope with her large family, 'Going from one child to five or six is really hard. I hope she's OK!'

They read each other's Household Manuals. To Tracey's dismay, Kate's suggests that there's a lot of housework, 'This lady has a very busy life!' Kate has her own problems – she's appalled to see that Tracey gets up at about 5.30am to do the ironing before getting Lottie up and then heading off to work. It's going to be an interesting swap…

Name: Tracey Bennett
Age: **36**   Status: **Married**
Occupation: **Legal Secretary**
Location: **Newcastle**
Children: **Lottie (4)**

Meet The Family

Tracey, though nervous, greets the Thomas family with a brave face. Trevor takes her through the daily routine in the kitchen, which is the centre of the household. On the fridge there is a list of which child does what and when, so everyone is clear what they have to do. The Thomas children are nice but rather a handful, especially as Trevor goes straight out to work, leaving her to get on with it on her first night. He offers her some tips, the most important being; in a large family you can't afford to concentrate on just one child at a time, you have to manage three simultaneously. Probably not what an already overwhelmed Tracey needs to hear. It's safe to say Trevor and Tracey haven't exactly hit it off, not least because the spaghetti that she had prepared earlier as an evening meal was stone cold by the time Trevor had finished showing her the house and detailing the children's routine and her duties. Not satisfied with his stand-in wife's grub, Trevor throws the whole thing into the dustbin and asks her to start again. Tracey's reaction? 'This is just a nightmare.' However, things are about to get even worse. As the house is so crowded, Tracey will be living in a caravan parked outside. She is given a walkie-talkie, just in case Trevor needs her to deal with kids during the night. Could things get any worse?

Name: Trevor Thomas
Age: 36
Occupation: Family Support Unit/Bouncer

By contrast, it's all going swimmingly in the Bennett household, as Kate immediately takes to her temporary family. Kate is delighted to receive a big hug from Lottie, exclaiming: 'I didn't expect you to be so affectionate!' Based on first impressions, someone's definitely got the better deal, but as we know by now, that can all change…

Getting To Know You…

It might only be a ten day swap, but before long Tracey feels completely isolated in her new home, bemoaning her fate with,

I feel that there's no light at the end of this tunnel.

Her problem is not just with Trevor, though she continues to find him not just irritating but overbearing: 'My first impression? He's so dictatorial.' She also has a problem with the children, who are a bit of a handful at the best of times, but quickly suss out that Tracey is

easily thrown off course by their combined antics, and unable to impose her will on them once she's wound up. The children comment, 'Tracey only says she is going to get angry, but she doesn't... she makes threats but then doesn't carry them out.' Sounds brilliant if you're eight, really...

On the contrary, Tracey does seem quite capable of expressing her anger at her new family's behaviour, but just not to them directly:

Bollocks to them! It's not fair that they play me up like this. I don't like it and I feel like saying bloody bugger off and do it yourself!

However, the experience does give her an insight into why Trevor seems to be a disciplinarian at home: 'Now I understand why Trevor is the way he is – if you lose control of them, you're stuffed!' The one threat that does seem to work is that she will tell Trevor they have been really naughty. At this the children soon seem to fall into line, each making sure that they get her to promise that she won't 'tell on' them to their father. Problem solved. Full marks to Tracey for ingenuity.

Kate meanwhile has a different sort of ordeal to cope with, in taking over Tracey's job at the law firm, which she finds a less than thrilling way to spend the day. Adding this to her back-breaking commute and the unearthly hour at which she had to start the day, Kate's new life is well and truly exhausting, as she tells Mark when she finally gets home:

My body feels alive, but my head feels dead. At home it's the other way around!

Mark nods sympathetically, but he's not very happy with Kate's approach to housework, which he thinks is sloppy.

Over at the Thomas' house, Tracey is also unhappy at the mess: 'It's disgusting, it's dirty, it's messy! I don't know how they live like it!' Kate has her criticisms too, namely of the way the Bagleys are raising their young daughter. Speaking of their practice of putting her

Try to make time for family activities, no matter how tired you are after work or at the weekend.

in day-care, she worries, 'I would have this huge sense of guilt if it was my daughter… I've got preconceived ideas about day care… it isn't something I've chosen for my own children, but then I suppose I haven't got such a good career.' It's certainly going to be interesting when the roles get reversed.

Turning The Tables

Both wives look forward to imposing their own rules in the new homes, but of the two it is Tracey whose changes are the most dramatic. She tells Trevor that she doesn't feel he supports her enough, and that he needs to appreciate just how much Kate actually does. From now on, he will get the children up in the morning and will be more considerate to her: she takes great exception to the fact that he doesn't pull out the plug after having a bath. Crucially, they will now swap places and Trevor will sleep in the caravan. After all, if he wants anything, he has a walkie talkie…

Would your heart sink if your guest room was a caravan? Keep your visitors' happy by at least installing running water!

Trevor agrees, but isn't happy: 'I feel disappointed that she feels my role in the family is minute compared to what Kate does.' He is still going to work in the evenings, and what with having far more child-care thrust on him, and a hostile woman in the house, work becomes something of a refuge.

Kate's changes centre on Lottie and the issue of how best to care for her. She decides to work part time, and takes some time off. She introduces an egg-timer, a device she considers to be a very useful tool for dealing with children and getting them into a routine. Mark isn't so sure, but is surprised to see that it works when it comes to Lottie brushing her teeth. The timer is set for one minute, and she cleans them for the whole 60 seconds: the most Mark and Tracey have managed with her is 20 seconds. Good on you, Kate.

Unfortunately, it's the twin issues of Lottie's teeth and the timer that cause relations between Mark and Kate to disintegrate. Kate wants to use it to limit Lottie's use of her dummy, which she is very attached to. Although Mark has agreed to play by Kate's rules, he over-rides her when it comes to this issue and after a fierce row Kate has to back down.

Mark confides to his video diary that he finds Kate's rules oppressive, ranting,

> *It's too much like being at boot camp. There's a series of stickers on the wall with stars for good behaviour. If you get enough you get a prize. It's too much like training a dog to do tricks.*

Although he describes Kate as 'a bit of a nag', there are some tactics which seem to work and Mark admits that she obviously has tricks up her sleeve when it comes to child-care. When bathing Lottie, Kate tells her not to do something, and to Mark's surprise his daughter backs down immediately. He and Tracey have so little time with Lottie, he admits, that they don't want the conflict of having to discipline her, so this is a real breakthrough for him.

Trevor and Tracey aren't getting on any better. Trevor feels that there may be a social issue here as well as a family one, deciding 'She feels she's a bit upper class for us'. Tracey meanwhile is having some moments of self-doubt, brought on by the unlikely catalyst of

Can you really keep a clean and tidy house with six children? Perhaps 'Bollocks to it!' is the way forward!

a spot of light cake-making. Confiding in her video diary after the baking session, she explains that the experience of the whole family making a cake together was very enjoyable on one level, but that she was so upset she couldn't speak when she realised that she had never made a cake with her own daughter. She starts to really worry that she is 'a crap mother.'

Taking Stock

The reunion proves to be a bumpy one. Kate protests that 'Lottie's voice has to be heard', and that it would be better if Tracey spent more time with her; preferably taking her out of nursery. In turn, a sensitive Tracey is furious that Kate is criticising the way she brings up her child, and hits back with a dig about the state of Kate's house. The fur really starts to fly as the two women lay into each other and a *Jerry Springer Show*-esque battle of vocal abuse ensues; 'Calm down, love', 'Don't even go there!', 'Don't point!', 'Don't shout!', 'That's very, very rude!' Tracey then tells Kate, 'I pity you!'

Well, don't! Send your pity to Oxfam!

comes the reply. Er, that went well, then.

The women's approach to life couldn't be more different and they seem to have little to say to each other. Tracey's furious and reacts strongly to the slightest criticism – a raw nerve has been exposed and Kate has managed to score a direct hit. The reunion, it's fair to say, has not been a great success.

The View From The Sofa

This was one of the most striking *Wife Swap* episodes. It was reminiscent of a Hitchcock movie: the composed blonde (Tracey) is sent away from her usual environment to another, where she is humiliated, bedraggled and finds herself in serious trouble. The contrast between the poised woman at home and the swearing, harassed woman trapped in a caravan that she hated made for great television.

The couples' reunion at the end was explosive, and the verbal cat-fight between the two wives was very entertaining. Both women had their most deep-seated worries brought out for public scrutiny. Kate's comments about child-raising were particularly hurtful to Tracey, who we had seen confessing her own self doubts on this score.

Kate seemed equally upset when it came to criticism of her home's cleanliness, and was perhaps a bit too forceful in her opinions on day care and on what was best for Lottie – the implication being that the little girl's interests were not being properly considered by her parents. To be fair to Tracey, that was a charge that any mother would have reacted very strongly to, especially on top of a knackering ten days in a stranger's home.

So how did we get on with the 'grass must be greener' theory? Well, neither woman enjoyed the other's lifestyle. Kate found both the job and commute very boring and tiring, while Tracey was exhausted and frustrated by the demands of looking after six children. Had she had a better rapport with Trevor things might have been more enjoyable, but even so she would have missed work, especially as being a career woman is such a major part of her self-image. Time will tell if the big issues that have been aired are brushed back under the carpet, or become a real catalyst for change in each household.

What The Papers Said

The third programme, in which mother of six Kate changes places with mother of one Tracey, is nowhere near as tortuous, although everyone involved does appear to be having a pretty dismal time. "Mark and I spent days getting Kate's room ready so she'd be comfortable," says Tracey at one point, "and what do I get? Stuck in a caravan in the garden."

The Guardian, 24 January, 2003

Music to Swap Wives By!

We reckon these are some of the top songs to swap wives by. Some were heard in the show and some we think you should have on the CD player when you really want to make a point to your partner!

1. Stuck in the Middle with You

2. Don't Marry Her

3. Our House

4. Nine to Five

5. We Are Family

6. Girls Just Wanna Have Fun

7. You Give Love a Bad Name

8. I Say A Little Prayer

9. Oops, I Did it Again

10. I Still Haven't Found What I'm Looking For

11. Shout!

12. Love and Marriage

13. Always Look on the Bright Side of Life

14. Back On the Chain Gang

15. I Just Don't Know What to Do With Myself

Series 1 Episode 4

WIFE SWAP

The Couples

Rob and Anne Bagley have been married for 18 years, and have two children, Jessica and Alice. Anne works as a manager with IKEA and prides herself on her organisational skills: she is a natural organiser with an eye for detail, and her job is important to her. Back at home, Rob does most of the housework, which is fine with Anne, though she adds ominously that 'he doesn't always do it to my standard'. Rob rather defensively says 'It's not that I'm under the thumb. If I didn't like it I'd say I didn't like it – but it works.' More positively, he describes them as 'trendy... a modern family.' They work well as a couple, but of the two it's Anne who is the stronger character.

Graham and Diane Kelly have been married for 23 years, and have two teenage children. Both run their own business: Graham has his own bakery. He does none of the housework, considering it to be Diane's responsibility. Graham believes in letting Diane get on with running the house: 'I don't think I do anything at home', he says, happily. Graham's clearly not the sort of man to arrive back home, put on a pinny and get on with a little light dusting. Diane's comment on housework is fairly clear;

Name: Rob Bagley
Age: 42
Occupation: Company Director

He doesn't believe in illness, if I broke my leg I'd still have to carry on.

Arriving

Anne looks forward to the swap as she arrives at the Kellys' house, because she hopes to be able to learn something useful. 'The opportunity of improving the way my household runs is very important to me. We're quite forward looking and I am always looking for ways to improve the efficiency of this house.' Her biggest fear is that someone will come into this house and run it more efficiently than I do.

I am perhaps a perfectionist who doesn't want anybody to be able to do anything better than I can.

Diane's approach is more down to earth, but she's more nervous of the experience than Anne is. It isn't looking after the children that concerns her, it's 'meeting the bloke. It's the husband that I'm more worried about'. For any woman, the idea of living in a house with another man is bound to be a bit intimidating. She hopes that the family she'll be living with for ten days is like her own, so there won't be too many drastic changes to her normal routine.

Both Anne and Diane find the process of looking round a stranger's house without its occupants very odd, embarrassing, even. When they read each other's Household Manuals, Anne is less than impressed as she doesn't think enough care has been taken over the answers to the various questions in the Manual. 'Maybe it's not somebody who's got the attention to detail.' Oh dear.

Anne goes through the Kellys' kitchen as if she's on an inspection rather than acting as a visitor, and as she does so she finds plenty to criticise: food is on the wrong shelf, there are dishes in the washing up bowl that need seeing to, she wants to clean a frying pan that's been left on the stove, When she gets upstairs to the master bedroom she finds a pile of magazines and other bits and pieces on the bedside table, 'I couldn't live like that' she comments.

Making her way around the Bagleys', Diane is more laid back, though she's thrown by the difference in family diet. Anne's top three dishes, she reads, are 'Pasta, fish and salad' then adds 'I've put curry, spaghetti bolognaise and anything in chips'. If the way to a man's heart is through his stomach, then Graham's is a traditional one. How will he cope with a woman whose idea of food is fancy salads? Will Diane's dishes be suitably modern and tangy for Rob and family?

Meet The Family

Anne meets Diane's family, including Diane's mother, Dorothy, who lives with them in a granny annexe. The introductions seem to go OK, and the two children, Joe and Tina, seem pleased to meet her. Over at the other house, Diane wants to show Rob and family pictures of her own children, but can't remember where she's put them. She rummages about for what seems like ages, though Rob and the kids aren't really that interested anyway, (looking at someone

Name: Diane Kelly
Age: 42 Status: Married
Occupation: Baker
Location: Stafford
Children: Joe (19), Tina (16)

else's family snapshots is never very exciting at the best of times) but Diane ploughs on regardless, though we get the impression that she doesn't actually find them. Or if she does, her hosts have collapsed with exhaustion while waiting.

Back in her room, Diane imagines that Graham will be uncharacteristically helpful with Anne, and that he'll no doubt revert to type when she gets home. She's right on one level, because he has been quite attentive in making her feel welcome. Anne, speaking to camera, seems to like Graham so far but wonders how long it will last: 'It would have been awful to just sort of walk in and not have any help or not be shown where things were. But judging by what Diane says in here [the Manual] he doesn't normally do much in the house, so we'll see what happens over the next few days, whether he sort of goes back to his normal routine where everything's done for him.' Both Anne and Graham seem to think the other is a decent person with whom they can get on, while Diane is also settling in happily, as she confides to the camera:

They're dead, dead nice, the kids are brilliant... Rob's brilliant... It's brill.

What could possibly go wrong?

Getting To Know You...

The start of the day is radically different in each household: Diane is woken with a cup of tea by the caring, sharing Rob. Anne is up on her own at 6am (Graham has already left for work) and she's expected to crack on with the housework before heading off for a full day at IKEA.

Given that she's used to that sort of punishing routine, Diane finds all this lying around and being waited on first thing in the morning rather hard to get used to. What is she for? If anything, she finds it frustrating that, compared to her day back home, she has so little to do: 'I've got no dog, the kids get themselves up and there's no housework for me to do because the cleaners are coming in.' She doesn't even have to make the kids' breakfast as they and their lodger make it before heading off for school, and Diane is left watching from the sidelines as the children politely look after themselves.

Are you married to the most chauvinistic man out of your group of friends?

The Devil makes work for idle hands, and Diane's lack of anything constructive to do – Rob has even got cleaners in so she won't have to worry about that side of the housework – means that she has time to do a little sniping at her new home. All this foreign food, for example. Surely it's a bit over the top? Exotic just for the sake of it?

I've never ate an olive...
They haven't got a plain one.
Some dried aubergines – I've never ate
an aubergine either... How big's a cod
fillet? Because I never buy fish...
There's some funny cheese in the
fridge as well... smells of old socks.

You get the impression that if she's going to have any cheese in her fridge, it'll be good, plain, straightforward cheddar. No old socks on her shelves, no siree.

At the Kellys', Anne, despite a good night's sleep, is already starting to bristle as she prepares dinner for the first evening: 'In my house Rob wouldn't just stand there watching me do everything; he'd actually get involved.' This comment comes after Graham, back from work, stands in the kitchen watching Anne prepare the evening meal. He watches, fascinated, as she moves around the kitchen. A big mistake. He sees it as showing a friendly interest in what she's doing: she sees it as incredibly rude that he's just standing there and not lifting a finger to help her. Graham, who, as we are beginning to suspect, is a man who knows his own mind, refuses to rise to the bait when Anne tells him about how Rob would make himself useful. 'Would he?' is all he says, literally standing his ground as she continues, on her own, to get the meal ready.

He may not be prepared to help with the cooking, but he's happy to chat away to Anne over dinner, trying to cheer her up with some of his ready humour. His daughter, Tina, is less than impressed with her Dad's efforts in this direction, as she tells the camera when alone in her bedroom: 'My Dad is showing off quite a lot. He's cracking bad jokes and I think she's a bit scared, She doesn't know whether to laugh or not at his jokes because they're not very funny.' At least he's trying to

> If housework keeps getting in the way, just don't do it every day! We've said it before, life is too damn short.

be funny. But if he's failing to amuse Tina he's also clearly not getting through to Anne. She would rather he had helped with the meal!

Things seem to be going rather better at the Bagleys' house, though conversation feels a bit forced. The highlight of the evening's chat over the dinner table seems to be when it is revealed that Rob, to the incredulity and amusement of his daughters, has bought the wrong colour toilet rolls. Their bathroom is decorated in white and cream, and Anne, when around, is very particular about colour schemes. The loo paper has to be exactly the right shade of cream. So why has Rob bought blue? Is he colour blind? Forgetful? Or is this meant to be an act of rebellion, a small but significant blow for artistic differences, a sign that his spirit hasn't been crushed?

Whatever the reason, the blue loo paper does at least enable Diane to observe that the Bagleys discuss domestic matters as a group, explaining 'That's a lot different from my house.' Hopefully her house has more interesting things to get amused and excited over, and for a moment the viewer can't help but feel that half an hour of Graham's bad jokes might be more fun that a full-scale inquest into the right shade of loo paper.

Do you always know where your kids are?
Check up on them once in a while to test
their creative excuse-making ability!

At the end of this exciting meal Rob, in his own room and to camera, confides that he thinks everything's going well. He hopes both families will, in future, keep in touch over the years, and look back fondly on the swap. Little does he realise…

At Graham's house things are going from bad to worse. Graham tells the camera that he thinks Anne is upset at not receiving more help with cooking the meal after she gets in from work… 'So I got the sense she was upset and that amused me slightly or unnerved me or something. Whereas yesterday I thought "oh, she's ever so pleasant, she's lovely", now I'm a little bit wary… 'He's right to be on his guard, because Anne is not a happy woman. Oh, no.

As the week goes on, Anne finds the combination of a full-time job and relentless housework very tiring. Graham tends to cycle off to work in a dashing, tour-de-France style outfit, at the unearthly hour of 5.30am, cheerfully leaving her to do the housework while the children are still asleep and before she starts work herself.

I feel like one of them cavemen who has got to protect their family and comes out with a big club.

Graham

Speaking of the children, Anne finds it unsettling that Tina, whom she ferries into town for a meeting with her friends, is deliberately vague about where she is going, and with which friend. Anne likes to know exactly where her children are and who they are with. There's definitely trouble a-brewing.

Diane, who is used to the routine that Anne is now lumbered with, finds it bizarre that Anne, when at home, has the time and energy – let alone the desire – to go to the gym. In fact, she thinks it's selfish: 'I wouldn't sort of think it right, "I'm going to an exercise class on a Wednesday and a Saturday and nobody's going to get in the way", because I've always got to prioritise and I would say I come last in the list.' The language that she uses in talking about Anne: selfishness, unstoppability, grim determination suggests that she's building up a very negative image of her. What will happen when the two wives come face to face?

For her part, Anne is equally perplexed by what she sees as Graham's slapdash attitude to where Tina is and when. Anne gets very fretful when she is five minutes late to be picked up, 'It seems

If you usually put yourself 'last in the list' make some time for a pampering session and LOCK THE BATHROOM DOOR!

to be a bit of a free for all, everybody does what they want and there doesn't seem to be the communication beforehand so that everybody knows where everybody else is.' Her own family are clearly much more regimented than Diane's, and she is as irritated at Diane's informality as Diane is at her career woman, have-it-all lifestyle.

Of the two, Diane seems to be having the better time, though she tells Rob that she's worried about her home; 'I think the whole of my house revolves around me. I'm the key to it and think if I'm not there she'll think "what a disorganised house". But basically if I'm there it works quite well.' What if Anne is actually running it as well or, heaven forbid, even better?

Graham and Anne also have a conversation, but it's a far less friendly one than Diane and Rob's fireside chat. Graham tries to explain his philosophy of family life; he does the hard work at the business, and his wife is there to see the children off in the morning, be there when they get back and cope with all domestic issues. It's a division of responsibilities that works for them, but which is all lost on Anne, who ends the night in her room with the camera. As far as she is concerned, Graham is the archetypal 'male chauvinist pig. He sat there tonight basically telling me that I'm a bad parent because I go to work and that a woman's place is in the home doing the housework. I just can't believe it.'

Turning the Tables

Anne can't wait to turn the tables on Graham, and kicks off, at a family gathering, with her desire to introduce a 'healthier' diet. Graham isn't happy, asking, 'Why d'you think we're unhealthy?' Hardly a case of embracing change or being willing to look at another way of doing things which is, after all, the whole point of getting involved in *Wife Swap* in the first place... Anne ignores his comment and briskly moves on to other issues. There's too much clutter for her taste. That'll have to stop. And as for the children going out with friends, well, she wants to know exactly where everyone is, who they are with, when and for how long.

Diane's changes, on the other hand, seem fairly uncontroversial. She cancels the weekly cleaner so that she can have the housework done by her own fair hand in her way. She wants to cut the clutter too, but in her case it isn't piles of magazines that she wants to dispose of, it's what she sees as bureaucratic household lists. Lists and notes are of course Anne's speciality, and she leaves a note for Graham, asking him to tidy his room, and to say that it is his son, Joe, who should do the cooking that night as she is going out. Graham solves the problem – and breaks the rules – by ordering a take-away pizza delivery. Tina rationalises this with 'Anne's not here so it doesn't really matter. She won't find out 'til she's gone, anyway.' It looks as if it's not just Graham, but the children who also resent Anne's new rules. There's dissent in the ranks already… it's going to be a long five days.

In fact, Anne does find out about Pizzagate. Much of the pizza is left in the carton, in a cupboard. It's almost as if the Kelly family hope that she'll find it and leaving it in the cupboard is an act of defiance! Not surprisingly, Anne is not pleased, and she has every right to be angry. She has played by the Kelly's rules and it's only fair (and is the agreed procedure) that, for the second half of the swap, they should play by hers.

Household Manual's
Series Two

WIFE SWAP

Jason & Nicola Episode 1

Household Chores

How often do you clean your home?

Every day. we have a cleaner once a week.

Who does the cleaning in general? Is this done voluntarily, or only when asked?

I do it all, apart from when the cleaner is here.

Who does the following, and how often...

Hoovering?
I do – once a week. Cleaner once a week.

Dusting?
I do it every weekend, thoroughly.
Cleaner dusts once a week.

Tidying?
I do – every day.

Ironing?
Cleaner – once a week.

Cleaning the bathroom?

I do every weekend.
Cleaner does it once a week.

Clothes washing?

I do – every other day. I don't have a washing line, I put everything in the tumble dryer.

DIY?
My dad, or pay someone.

Decorating?
I do – I'm always doing new things to the house.

Other / what?
I sweep the floors every day, except when the cleaner is here. I wash the floors every other day. At the weekend I clean everything thoroughly – windows, tops of units, mirrors, door frames and unit doors. I never use polish – I use wood cleaner and glass cleaner. I change all the bedding every weekend.

Every day I let out the chicken and the cockerel. During the night they'll go back into their pens of their own accord. I also rake the grass outside the pen every other day, and give them fresh food and water every morning. Once a week I'll clean out the cage. I'll leave the gate open so they go out as I'm cleaning. (The spray I use and the instructions are out, but usually there is spray that's already made up).

Extra House Rules?

I don't allow anyone to wear shoes on the upstairs carpets, and no smoking is allowed anywhere except the kitchen, though Jason is allowed to smoke in his office.

I always make sure that the outside gate to the main road is closed. I also tighten all the taps as Morgan tries turning them on.

Where do you eat?

In the kitchen. We use the dining room when have friends round at the weekend.

When are meal times?

The kids and I eat between 5pm and 6pm. My partner eats between 7pm and 8pm depending when he gets home.

Who prepares breakfast / lunch / dinner?

I do. I prepare my son's lunch every morning – sandwiches, crisps, Babybell cheese, Dairylea Dunkers, Pepperami, yoghurt, chocolate bars. I try to keep it different every day, interesting and elaborate. I have to hide everything I buy for my son's lunch each week, because otherwise the family will eat it all.

Does your partner help?

doesn't really either. The kids like biscuits and cakes – treats. My daughter has to have full-fat cream milk every morning and night in a bottle.

How often do you get take-away's?

Varies. Once or twice on the weekend, sometimes during the week.

How often do you go out to eat?

Tends to be on the weekend, roughly every other week.

Shopping (Food / Household Goods)

Who does the shopping for food and household goods?

Household Chores

How often do you clean your home?

I do a big clean once a week on a Friday, at about 11am after my telly programmes. This means thoroughly cleaning the bathroom and mopping the kitchen floor with bleach. I give the kitchen floor a once-over sometimes during the week and a sweep. I may vacuum every day depending on the state of it, I give the bathroom sink a once over every day and the loo seat.

Who does the cleaning in general? Is this done voluntarily, or only when asked?

I do – although Dave helps. He does all the washing up.

Who does the following, and how often...

Hoovering?
I do – every day.

Dusting?
I do – every other day.

Tidying?
My husband does.

Ironing?
I do – three times a week. I will save up about four loads of washing and do it all together. I hang it up or put it away straight away. My husband will iron something if I'm too busy.

Cleaning the bathroom?
I clean the bathroom thoroughly on a Friday, then wipe it over as and when during the week.

Clothes washing?
I do one or two loads a day. I usually do this at night while I'm watching television. After the load has finished I fold it up wet in the basket ready for hanging the next day.

I don't use the tumble dryer unless it's bad weather, I prefer to use the line, which is in the yard.

Cleaning the kitchen?
My husband cleans it but I mop the floor on a Friday with bleach.

Washing up?
My husband.

Loading the dishwasher?
We haven't got one.

Cleaning the car?
We haven't got one.

Gardening?
I sweep the yard every day because of the rabbit droppings. I don't go out the front.

DIY?
I do all the DIY, unless it's electrics. He's good with videos, TVs etc.

Decorating?
I do all the decorating, I'm really into it. I do ask his opinion and listen to what he says. My hobby is stencilling and distressing wooden things and furniture that I get from the charity shop where I volunteer. I keep the things for the DIY in the shed.

Pets?
We have a rabbit that has a thorough clean on Friday because that's when the bin men come. They can take away the droppings to stop them from smelling during the week.

First of all you have to take the rabbit out and let it run around the yard. Take all the messy straw out and put it in a carrier bag, spray disinfectant in the toilet area which is where the sawdust was. Let the disinfectant dry. Replace sawdust in the toilet area and put fresh hay in the bed area. Freshen up the sawdust and hay during the week if it gets wet and smelly.

The rabbit is let out when I'm in, he's very tame (Flossie). I give it pellets (feed) every morning while the kids have their breakfast and every evening at tea time.

Cooking / Meals

How often do you sit down and eat together?

Every night.

Where do you eat?

At the kitchen table.

When are meal times?

The kids eat breakfast at around 7.45am. I'll have my breakfast after I've dropped them off at school. We usually eat our tea between 5pm and 6pm. We have take-away's on Friday and Saturday night and Burger King on Saturday lunch times. The kids have free lunches at school.

Who prepares breakfast / lunch / dinner?

I get breakfast ready for the kids. My husband does everything else.

Does your partner help?

He is on his training course by the time they get up otherwise he would do breakfast as well.

Who cooks and when?

He does all the cooking. I do not cook.

What are your favourite dinners?

His favourite meals to cook are: pie and chips, sausage and mash, spaghetti bolognaise and a Sunday roast.

Do you all like eating similar sorts of food?

My son is a bit picky, he doesn't like roast chicken only chicken nuggets. I don't like curry, but my husband and my daughter do. The kids aren't mad on veg but we do try to get them to eat sweetcorn, peas etc. For pudding they'll have a yoghurt or an ice cream. They drink pop. Me and my husband drink about 20 cups of coffee each per day.

Do you have any special dietary requirements? Is there anything you won't eat?

My husband doesn't eat any fish apart from cod.

How often do you get take-away's?

We get take-away's on Friday and Saturday nights. It's either a kebab and chips which is so big we can share it between four or a pizza. Dave goes to get it and pays for it out of his own money.

Shopping (Food / Household Goods)

Who does the shopping for food and household goods?

I usually do it on a daily basis, but my husband will get bits in. Because he does all the cooking he will go and get a joint for the Sunday dinner or a bag of spuds because they are too heavy for me to carry.

Does your partner help?

Yes, he will go to the shop if we're missing stuff for the evening meal.

How often do you go food / household goods shopping?

I go to the supermarket every day, getting milk or bread and anything else we need. I don't really do a weekly shop. I talk to my husband about what he fancies cooking and check to see what we're running out of.

Household Chores

How often do you clean your home?

Colin cleans the home properly on Tuesday's and Thursday's.

Who does the cleaning in general? Is this done voluntarily, or only when asked?

Emma does the tidying and Colin cleans.

Who does the following, and how often...

Hoovering?
Emma will do some in the evenings and Colin will do it again properly twice a week.

Dusting?
Colin.

Tidying?
Emma.

Ironing?
Emma.

Cleaning the bathroom?
Colin.

Clothes washing?
Emma puts the washing in and Colin empties it.

Cleaning the kitchen?
This is Colin's domain!

Washing up?
Emma will tidy up after meals.

Loading the dishwasher (if applicable)?
Emma loads the dishwasher.

Cleaning the car?
Colin takes the cars to the garage.

Gardening?
Neither of us.

DIY?
Colin does it all.

Decorating?
Both of us.

Cooking / Meals

How often do you sit down and eat together?

We eat together every evening apart from Monday's, Friday's and Saturday's.

Where do you eat?

Pub carvery type places.

When are meal times?

4:30pm.

Who prepares breakfast / lunch / dinner?

Colin gets up at 7:30am and makes tea. He then prepares breakfast and dinner for everyone while the girls and Emma are getting ready.

Does your partner help?

Yes – he does most of the work.

Who cooks and when?

Colin.

What are your top three dinners?

Spaghetti bolognaise, lasagne, roast.

Do you all like eating similar sorts of food?

Emma likes more basic things – will eat anything put in front of her. Colin is into spicy dishes.

Do you have any special dietary requirements? Is there anything you won't eat?
No.

How often do you get take-away's?
About three nights per week on average. It's usually a treat.

Shopping (Food / Household Goods)

Who does the shopping for food and household goods?
Colin does all the food shopping.

How often do you go food / household goods shopping?
Colin does it three times a week.

Lizzie & Mark Episode 2

Household Chores

How often do you clean your home?
Every day. On Saturday I do the kids' rooms.

Who does the cleaning in general? Is this done voluntarily, or only when asked?
Everyone mucks in, but Mark does the most.

Who does the following, and how often...

Hoovering?
Mark, as I was always pregnant.

Dusting?
Mostly Mark.

Tidying?
Mostly Mark.

Ironing?
I do this as and when needed –

Cleaning the bathroom?
Mostly Mark.

Clothes washing?
Lizzie.

Cleaning the kitchen?
Lizzie.

Washing up?
I do the pots and pans only.

Loading the dishwasher?
Elliot – oldest child.

Cleaning the car?
Mark.

Gardening?
Mark.

DIY?
Mark.

Decorating?
Both of us.

Cooking / Meals

How often do you sit down and eat together?

We eat together every night. Parents and older children eat off their lap's in front room. Little kids eat at the table in the kitchen.

Where do you eat?

Living room and kitchen.

When are meal times?

Breakfast: 7.30am to 8.15am
Lunch: 12.45pm
Dinner: 3.45pm to 6pm

Who prepares breakfast / lunch / dinner?

I do, but Casey helps.

Does your partner help?

Only if asked.

Who cooks and when?

I cook every meal.

What are your top three dinners?

All from scratch, potato hash, spaghetti bolognese, shepherds pie, lasagne.

Do you all like eating similar sorts of food?

Yes.

Do you have any special dietary requirements? Is there anything you won't eat?

No.

How often do you get take-away's?

Once a week, pizza and Indian. Twice a week, sandwiches for lunch.

Shopping (Food / Household Goods)

Who does the shopping for food and household goods?

I do.

Does your partner help?

Yes, he pushes the trolley.

Household Chores

How often do you clean your home?

Everyone has chores that they are responsible for. It is a shared house. We keep it clean and tidy together.

I do not use any chemical cleaners or polish in the house. We clean the surfaces in the kitchen with a mixture of Ecover (washing up liquid) and we clean the floors with a mixture of lavender oil and Ecover. Bleach is only allowed to be used in the toilet.

Who does the cleaning in general? Is this done voluntarily, or only when asked?

My daughters Jess (14) and Asher (16) alternate cleaning of the bathroom and the kitchen on a daily basis. They are responsible for cleaning their own rooms. Asher does her own washing. Jess does a lot of the cleaning, she will hoover and tidy. My son Joel, (12) unloads and loads the dishwasher in the morning, Jess and Asher take turns doing that in the evening. My partner Raff will hoover and cleans and tidies the house if I am at work. Raff does his own ironing. The children will fold up the washing. Raff will hang it out. I do the rest.

Who does the following, and how often...

Hoovering?

If Raff is here in the morning and has time he will do it or I do it at the weekend. Jess will do it when she comes in from school. I wash the floors regularly during the week.

Dusting?

Jess and I do it.

Tidying?

Everybody must tidy – I crack the whip when I come in. Joel is not allowed to play out until his room is tidy. If there are things to do I delegate.

Ironing?

Everyone does their own except Joel. I do my ironing and his on a Monday evening. Raff does his own ironing.

Cleaning the bathroom?

Asher and Jess clean the bathroom on alternate days.

Clothes washing?

Every day. Everyone puts clothes in the laundry bag by the bathroom. I usually put the washing in and Raphael will hang it out if he's here, either on the line or on the radiators depending on the weather. The kids will fold the washing. You need to chase Joel to put clothes in bag otherwise it builds up. Asher does her own washing.

Cleaning the kitchen?

If Raphael is here in the morning he cleans the kitchen and puts some washing on. Jess and Asher alternate keeping the kitchen clean on a daily basis.

Washing up?

We use a dishwasher.

Loading the dishwasher (if applicable)?

Joel is responsible for loading and unloading the dishwasher in the morning. The girls are responsible for doing it in the evenings.

Cleaning the car?

Only once a year.

Gardening?

I do the front garden and water the window boxes, dead-head the flowers, pick out weeds and sweep path, once a week. Raff cuts the grass once a week in the back garden and I weed.

DIY?

Raff

Decorating?

I do it with Raff.

Other / what?

I use the juicer twice each day. Asher and I clean the juicer when on kitchen duty.

Cooking / Meals

How often do you sit down and eat together?

Most nights we eat together, organic, vegetarian (although we do have fish) meals that I cook from scratch. On Sunday's I always make a big family dinner that we eat together at 6pm.

Where do you eat?

At the dining room table.

When are meal times?

Dinner is from 6.30pm to 7pm.

Who prepares breakfast / lunch / dinner?

Everyone makes their own breakfast. I always have porridge and juice for breakfast. Joel has a packed lunch every day which is made by either me or Raff (Raff will make if he's off work). I prepare my packed lunch in the morning, which is usually a brown rice salad made with pulses and salad. I have wheat once a week. Dinner is shared between either me or Raff depending on who is in first, but it's usually me.

Does your partner help?

I do more of the cooking but he helps out. I usually do it all at the weekend.

Who cooks and when?

No absolute rule, but I usually do more. Raff will cook if in before me.

What are your top dinners?

Fried marinated tofu followed by vegan Thai curry. Fried Fish, rice and peas, steamed plantain, salad and vegetables. Baked salmon with vegetables, peppers, carrots, potatoes, onions and garlic and brown rice. Organic pizzas, baked potatoes, salad and broccolli. We ALWAYS eat veg and salad with every meal.

Do you all like eating similar sorts of food?

Yes. Only one meal is cooked for the whole family.

Do you have any special dietary requirements? Is there anything you won't eat?

No dairy. No meat – only fish. Everything is organic. No alcohol. No caffeine. Two freshly squeezed organic juices a day; one veggie, one fruit. Supplements.

How often do you get take-away's?

Once a week only. I have Pad Thai. Asher, Jess and Joel are allowed what they want. Raff has West Indian.

Shopping (Food / Household Goods)

Who does the shopping for food and household goods?

I do the shopping because I know what organic produce I want. Raff will help.

Does your partner help?

Yes.

How often do you go food / household goods shopping?

I go to the organic greengrocers twice a week. Once a week I go to Sainsburys.

Household Chores

How often do you clean your home?

I clean, tidy, cook, wash up, do the laundry and sweep the floors every day.

Who does the cleaning in general? Is this done voluntarily, or only when asked?

I do everything.

Who does the following, and how often...

Hoovering?
I do, every day.

Dusting?
I do, once a week.

Tidying?
I do, every day.

Ironing?
I do, twice a week on Sunday and Thursday.

Cleaning the bathroom?
I do, a wipe round after every bath and then properly once a week.

Clothes washing?
I do a wash every day. The laundry basket is at the top of the stairs.

Cleaning the kitchen?
I do it every day. The cooker gets cleaned thoroughly once a week.

Washing up?
I do it every day.

Loading the dishwasher (if applicable)?
Haven't got one.

Gardening?
Justin.

DIY?
Justin.

Decorating?
Justin.

Other / what?
Rubbish goes out every day in the front yard. Kids have a bath every day at 7.30pm.

Cooking / Meals

How often do you sit down and eat together?

The kids eat together in front of the TV, then I cook something for Justin and me later. We hardly ever eat together as a family apart from at the weekends.

Where do you eat?

On our laps on the sofas.

When are meal times?

Amy and Antonella help themselves in the morning. Amy will make Dre's cereal or toast depending on what she is having. I don't really have lunch during the week. The kids have their tea at 6.30pm, we eat after that.

Who prepares breakfast / lunch / dinner?

The kids help themselves to breakfast, I prepare all meals. Justin will not touch a kitchen utensil.

Does your partner help?

No unless it's going to McDonalds.

Who cooks and when?

What are your top three dinners?

McDonalds, chicken tikka masala out of the jar (Justin has only just started eating this), sausage and mash, shepherds pie and chips.

Do you all like eating similar sorts of food?

Pretty much. Except Justin won't eat salad, vegetables or anything spicy.

Do you have any special dietary requirements? Is there anything you won't eat?

Justin doesn't eat any salad or veg.

How often do you get take-away's?

About four times a week.

Shopping (Food / Household Goods)

Who does the shopping for food and household goods?

I do the shopping. Justin and kids will come with me at weekends.

Does your partner help?

He can come with me at weekends.

How often do you go food / household goods shopping?

Once a week but with extra bits. I get milk delivered.

Nigel & Deborah Episode 4

Household Chores

How often do you clean your home?

My husband and I believe in operating a shared household, we are both hardworking with our own businesses. However, because our family home is also my bed and breakfast business it's easy for

Who does the cleaning in general? Is this done voluntarily, or only when asked?

I do more of the cleaning as the bed and breakfast is my business.

Who does the following, and how often...

Hoovering?

Tidying?
Every day as above. Nigel has a fantastic eye for detail.

Ironing?
I do the ironing every other day, often in front of the TV, or whilst chatting to Nigel.

Cleaning the bathroom?
I clean the guest bathrooms every day. They need to be spotless. I clean our own bathroom every three to four days and again it depends on how busy I am. Nigel will also keep an eye on all the bathrooms to make sure they are OK.

Clothes washing?
Our family laundry tends to get done on a daily basis with the B&B sheets, etc.

Cleaning the kitchen?
I do. Thoroughly every day.

Washing up?
I do. Every day.

Loading the dishwasher?
The boys will help.

Cleaning the car?
Everyone cleans their own car.

Gardening?
A gardener comes in once a month to mow the lawn. I tend to go out into the garden once a month. I also water the hanging baskets three times a week (depending on rainfall.) Also dead-head the roses. Keep weeds down in the drive. Keep paths clean. Brush down paving stones.

DIY?
Nigel will do the necessary DIY jobs around the house. This is an on-going process.

Decorating?
Decorating is done once every four years and we hire professionals to do this.

Other / what?
I clean my bedroom as often as I can.

Karl and Aaron are to tidy and clean their own rooms. They are not good at this and if I've got the energy I'll try and get them to tidy. I often say "Shit heap! Clean it!" But it seldom works.

Swimming Pool: a woman comes once a week. Usually in the evenings.

Every morning during breakfast make sure that the fountain is turned on. (Nigel will explain.) Also that the sun loungers are set up.

Digby the Dog. He eats at about 7pm; half a dog sausage with four slices of toast plus scraps from breakfast. Please ensure his water bowl doesn't run dry during the day. He likes a bowl of warm tea after breakfast. Brush gently every other day (his brush is in the cupboard under the sink). He is not allowed upstairs.

Cooking / Meals

How often do you sit down and eat together?

There always seems to be at least one person missing from the table. Nigel and I tend to sit down to eat together most nights. I always cook a meal for Nigel and almost always for Karl and his girlfriend Nikki (or a friend). So plan for four people and try and get some sense out of Aaron to see what he's doing (he rarely has dinner with us). Be prepared for last minute additions though as friends or girlfriends may turn up.

Where do you eat?

Meals are eaten in the kitchen's breakfast area. Nigel and I will occasionally eat in the sitting room but the boys are not allowed to eat there because they make a mess.

When are meal times?

This is flexible and guests are taken into account.

Who prepares breakfast / lunch / dinner?

I do all the cooking in the house. Although Aaron is training to cook he never does any at home and eats a lot of take-away's.

Does your partner help?

Nigel helps out if and when needs be (emergencies only).

Who cooks and when?

See above.

What are your top three dinners?

Roast dinners, grilled salmon and salad. Chinese take away. Minced beef with mashed potatoes.

Do you all like eating similar sorts of food?

Karl and Aaron do not like vegetables.

Do you have any special dietary requirements? Is there anything you won't eat?

Not within the family. However we may get vegetarian guests that we will have to accommodate.

How often do you get take-away's?

If I have had a really busy week I will order take-away at least once a week. If Karl and Aaron have friends around then they normally get KFC.

Shopping (Food / Household Goods)

Who does the shopping for food and household goods?

I do.

Does your partner help?

Nigel likes to lend a hand when he is not at work.

How often do you go food / household goods shopping?

It all depends on how busy the B&B is. On average there is a shop done three to four times a week (depending on how many people are staying.)

Do a family shop once a week but often go out to pick up extras. Do a wholesale shop once a week. Some items are bought in bulk.

Always take the phone and then diary with you in case of bookings. Nigel will explain how to divert phone calls from the house.

Household Chores

How often do you clean your home?

I do a big clean once a week on a Wednesday. I start cleaning at 1pm and finish around 5pm. During this time I clean the bathroom, mop bathroom floor, mop the floor boards, sponge down kitchen surfaces, hoover everywhere, dust and polish, clean windows, wipe tops, clean top of cooker, clean grill pan, clean fridge, wipe kitchen doors and bleach sink. Wash laundry (clothes, towels, sheets) and hang out washing in-between cleaning. Every day we do general tidying, put away toys, wash up pots (no dishwasher). Stephen makes the bed, puffs the cushions on the sofa and puts the toys away.

Who does the cleaning in general? Is this done voluntarily, or only when asked?

I do. Stephen makes the bed when he wakes up in the morning, after he has had a coffee (he is, after all, the last one up). He straightens and puffs cushions and tidies away the kids toys.

Who does the following, and how often...

Hoovering?
I do. Stephen might, once in a blue moon! The living room is hoovered every other day by me.

Dusting?
I do. (Done on Wednesday's.)

Tidying?
I do. Stephen likes to puff and arrange cushions.

Ironing?
Stephen irons his own clothes and I do everyone else's. No-one is allowed to touch Stephen's clothes.

Cleaning the bathroom?
I do (as part of the thorough clean-up on Wednesday). Stephen does rinse the bath out after he has used it!

Clothes washing?
I do all the clothes washing (most days) but no-one is allowed in Stephen's football bag. I can wash hit football kit, but no-one is allowed to iron it.

Cleaning the kitchen?
I clean the kitchen. General washing every day, more thoroughly on Wednesday. Every day I wipe tops, wash pots, put washing on if clothes need cleaning.

Washing up?
Stephen does dinner dishes (but not at weekends). I do all the other dishes.

Cleaning the car?
Stephen – once a month at a car wash.

Gardening?
Have pub gardener.

DIY?
Stephen has a go, but often makes things worse. I often have to pay someone else.

Decorating?
Both of us, but it's mostly me. Stephen's not happy about doing decorating except for painting.

Other / what?
The pub has cleaners. I also do a bit of detailed cleaning like polishing and dusting the dado rail. Stephen tends to wander around behind the cleaners straightening ashtrays and chairs. The green stool by the bar is always Stephen's stool.

Cooking / Meals

How often do you sit down and eat together?

Every night. We have dinner on our laps while watching TV. There's never any conversation. Sometimes we go out to eat, but very rarely.

We never eat together at weekends. This is because Stephen drinks in the pub downstairs or if he is upstairs then I am usually behind the bar.

We are like passing ships at weekends. The kids and I eat together at weekends, roughly 5pm. Stephen will often go without eating at weekends, as he has been drinking.

Where do you eat?

In the living room on our laps. Mitchell has his own little chair and table in the living room.

When are meal times?

5pm. Steve likes a set time. Weekends are more relaxed.

Who prepares breakfast / lunch / dinner?

Breakfast: I make a basic breakfast for the kids. (Stephen asleep.)
Lunch: Steve eats alone upstairs. I will grab a sandwich in the pub. On Wednesday's and at weekends I make lunch for the kids, Stephen and myself. The rest of the time Stephen will make lunch (sandwich) for himself and the kids only.
Dinner: I do. (I often have to make three sets of meals.)
At weekends Steve won't eat lunch but I make him something anyway because he wants to have the option.

Does your partner help?

Never. (I can't remember the last time Stephen made me a cup of tea.)

Who cooks and when?

I do. After finishing my first shift at 4pm, I come upstairs to prepare dinner.

What are your top three dinners?

Jessica and Linda: Scouse (recipe contained in full Household Manual), spaghetti bolognese, chicken salad and jacket potato.

Stephen: He likes chicken and mushroom pie, spicy chicken and curries, chinese chicken and rice, potatoes. Stephen loves Sui Mai (pork steamed bought from chip shop) and stale bread.
Mitchell: fussy eater. He loves Thomas the Tank Engine ham, noodles, chips, chicken nuggets – anything you can get down him.

Do you all like eating similar sorts of food?

No. Steve and Mitchell are quite fussy, so I often make one meal for Jessica and I, one for Steve and another one for Mitchell.

Do you have any special dietary requirements? Is there anything you won't eat?

Stephen: no chips, no veg, no roast dinners. Stephen's mum will often bring roast dinner down for everyone but Steve – heat up in microwave. This happens every now and then.

How often do you get take-away's?

Maybe once a week, or if the pub is really busy (this is more of a treat).

If Steve has had a couple of drinks and he is hungry he will go to the chip shop for himself.

Shopping (Food / Household Goods)

Who does the shopping for food and household goods?

I do.

Does your partner help?

No. he does sometimes carry the shopping bags up the stairs, but you need to call him on the mobile and then he will come downstairs.

How often do you go food / household goods shopping?

Once a week, after cleaning.

Wearing the shirt you cleaned the floor with due to lack of laundry skills is not a good look, so if you don't know how to use that washing machine, now is the time to learn!

Anne's husband, Rob, isn't all that happy with his new diet, either. Diane introduces his girls to a more old-fashioned menu involving lots of potatoes. Watching them wolf down the stodge makes her happy, and as she cleans up after them in the kitchen, she tells the camera that 'Rob found it too stodgy, but the girls seemed to like it', and, more to the point, perhaps, 'I enjoyed it!' Her next big change is to encourage the Bagley daughters to mix more with their friends at home, and to do so in a less regimented fashion. Dispatching Rob to the gym, where he can pedal and push to his heart's content, Diane organises a party for the girls and their friends. She has to push them into playing along with the idea, but eventually they go into action, invite friends round, and everyone has a good time.

Diane is pleased at the result, because she feels the girls need a more informal approach to seeing and entertaining their friends. She feels it's too restrictive to have to book in a date when they can ask friends over to the house, saying of Anne, sarcastically, that 'when you're that organised, I suppose, they probably have to book it six months beforehand. 'And while Diane has a softer spot for Rob, it's blended with a certain mild contempt. She feels that Rob, though nice, is actually too nice. 'I think he's got no "go" in him, has he?' Though he has yet to meet him, and hasn't discussed the matter with Diane, Graham feels much the same about Anne's husband. He's sure he must be put-upon, given how bossy Anne seems, saying

Whenever I get to meet Rob the first thing I'll be looking for is a thumbprint on his head…

Relations between Graham and Anne sink to an all-time low when she tries to get him (and the rest of the family, including Joe's girlfriend) to eat some salad. Anyone would think she'd asked them to become cannibals for a day. Graham makes great play of the fact that he's actually eating the stuff, as normally his greens are limited to peas and perhaps a couple of sprouts. If he wants variety in his veg he goes crazy and has some carrots on the side. Speaking afterwards to camera, Anne – who finds this sarcastic lack of enthusiasm even more annoying than general refusal to lift a finger – says 'Graham's doing my head in… he's just very set in his ways. I think to start with I thought Diane was maybe quite a dominant character who just liked to do everything herself, but now I think she has to do it because Graham won't.'

She doesn't accept criticism very well, does she?
Graham on Anne

Graham, who is feeling the strain himself, phones Diane for a bit of moral support, and Diane not surprisingly takes his side. Graham does at least make the point that Anne is entitled to ask him to do things her way in the second week. 'I said I'd agree to live in her way this week, you know I'm a man of my word.' He is, and he follows the letter of the new law (other than that take-away pizza incident) but he's certainly not getting into its spirit.

Taking Stock

Things don't improve over the rest of the swap, though much to the viewing nation's disappointment, there are no more confrontations or shouting matches. The full extent of the mutual antagonism between the wives – however politely expressed – becomes clear at the reunion, where the couples meet each other for the first time. The animosity between Anne and Graham bursts forth, much to the surprise of Rob, who for his part had thought that the swap went well and was a pleasantly diverting experience.

Diane asks, mischievously, 'You don't want to keep Graham, then, Anne?' But Anne gives as good as she gets, and knows how to wind up Diane, by criticising the way she and her husband regulate their children's behaviour. She starts to say 'Nobody seems to know what anybody else is…' only to be cut off by Diane's 'Oh, I know. I know exactly what everybody's doing in my house.' Diane's steel, normally disguised under a jolly exterior but gradually revealed to the viewer via her asides to camera in the course of the swap, shines through.

After the reunion both couples talk over the experience, and Anne is clearly annoyed that Rob didn't back her up in public more, but Rob, never a man to embrace conflict, plaintively says he hadn't really noticed much tension. Graham and Diane share their dislike of Anne, who they characterise as 'bossy'. They come to the conclusion that Anne won't have learned any lessons from her time with them.

Rob does, eventually, show that he's taken on board Anne's dislike of Graham. In contrast to his high hopes, early in the swap, of continued friendship over the years, he says firmly that 'We haven't got enough in common to remain friends.' And the narrator closes

*I think she's like
wonderwoman in a leotard*
Diane on Anne

the programme by saying 'A few days later Graham called Anne to apologise for upsetting her and to invite the Bagleys for a drink with himself and Diane. His offer was politely declined.' Enough said.

The View From The Sofa

This episode proved to be the least sparky of series one of *Wife Swap*, but it still had useful things to say about relationships and how families operate. Anne and Diane were in many ways similar: both middle class and with similar sized families, but what the programme showed was that even among apparently like-for-like people, the way they run their households is very different. Their family rules, they way they relate to their husbands and children, the things they consider self-evidently 'normal' and right, are undoubtedly going to be very different.

Both women thought the way the other woman acted to be unreasonable or wrong, and the ill-feeling extended beyond the programme to the extent of the refusal to meet up socially after the reunion. Graham did indeed come across as a chauvinistic character, and became progressively more smug-looking as he spoke to the camera, but Anne too waged a continual war.

At the Bagleys' household Diane got on alright with Rob, though she found him a bit wet, but she became increasingly irritated, at one remove, with Anne, taking a growing dislike to the way she ran her house, let alone to what she might be doing to the family back at her home. Although there were none of the screaming matches that had made Sonia and Dee's swap such rivetting viewing, it was worth watching just for the moment when Diane voiced the the thoughts of many when she declared 'This feng shui is a waste of space'. As a result the programme came across as low key, but the viewing figures continued to rise sharply after it, and it proved that even with rather less dramatic characters than episode one, the concept and format of the show was easily strong enough to make for an interesting and involving programme.

What The Papers Said

Yet again there are some excruciating moments that will have you watching through your fingers, but even then you'll still recoil at some totally jaw-dropping comments. "Mum does all the work because we've usually got something better to do," says Diane's daughter. Hmm, and your mum doesn't? "There's no time for all this discussing in the Kelly household," says husband Graham, "because the dinner's burning."

Radio Times, 25-31 January, 2003

THE WIFE SWAP QUIZ, PART 3

Ladies, how good are your children?

1. You don't want them to have a pet hamster, as they didn't look after the last one. Do they...

a) nod understandingly and vow to be more responsible in future?

b) sulk?

c) scream four-letter abuse at you and stamp around the house for hours, slamming doors?

2. You ask them to make dinner one night. Do they...

a) surprise you with a beautifully-prepared three-course meal?

b) make the effort, though you have to be diplomatic about the results?

c) forget and order a take-away?

3. What sort of household chores do they do?

a) An equal share of the cleaning and helping with the shopping if you're busy.

b) They grudgingly polish the bathroom mirror now and again.

c) Most of the household shouting, and a good deal of its screaming and breaking of stuff.

4. How do they behave with each other?

a) They are the best of friends, loving and supportive.

b) They get along OK, with occasional bouts of yelling, punching and tears.

c) They refuse to acknowledge the human rights or indeed the very existence of siblings.

KEY

Mostly A's: These are imaginary children, aren't they?

Mostly B's: Don't worry, they'll grow up and leave home eventually.

Mostly C's: Have you considered hiring a nanny? Ex-KGB officers and former Marines are surprisingly affordable.

Swappers United

WIFE SWAP

New Wives, New Lives

The couples who volunteered for the first series of *Wife Swap* did so to find out what they could learn about their own lives by experiencing how other people lived their's. Given that it has been over a year since the first series was filmed, and the events that we watched took place, what have the original group of contributors learnt?

How have their lives changed? And has it been for the better? The reunion show, *Wife Swap Changed My Marriage*, casts some new light on the eight families involved and we spoke with them to see what they really think about their *Wife Swap* experience.

One of the best-known couples was Dee and Dave Jackson, the co-stars of the first episode. Even during the course of the ten days that they swapped lives with Lance and Sonia, it was clear that Dave had re-thought the way that he interacted with the other three members of his family – wife Dee and daughters Mary and Carol.

Speaking a year on, Dave is in no doubt that the swap had a great effect on family life, and that it was entirely for the good.

Wife Swap *showed us the error of our ways, and was very helpful in suggesting to us the things that we needed to do as a family.*

His first impression of Sonia, his temporary wife, had been less than encouraging: and he told Sonia that his wife was opposed to 'mixed marriages' which she took to mean that neither of them liked black people.

Sonia now says that she was aware of Dave's feelings about her colour as soon as she met him, but that she decided not to let it become an issue between them, or a problem for her. As viewers saw at the time, she sailed through that particular obstacle course by simply ignoring it, even during some hair-raising rows. The real problem was, and remained, the relationship between Dave and his daughters, with Sonia lining up on Dave's side and getting him to back her up, as part of her overall strategy to change the fact that they didn't respect him. Daughter Mary now agrees that she behaved badly and that she came across on the show as immature.

As a family, however, the Jacksons clearly get on a lot better now and Dee says that not only does she do far more housework than she used to (indeed, she does the majority of it now), but Dave really does stand up for himself a lot more. 'My going away for ten days seems to have done him a power of good.' Judging by the way he sings, 'Heaven, I'm in heaven' as she presses him to her ample bosom while combing his hair, it certainly appears so.

The Jacksons now go out together regularly and have a family meeting to discuss any issues that arise – such as buying another pet or keeping on top of tidying the cluttered flat that Sonia did her best to revamp. Surprisingly, Dee seems to like the relatively minimalist living room that awaited her on returning from the swap.

Her love of pets is still in evidence though and the family live with a mini zoo in the front room. In the update, the Jacksons discuss whether or not to add a rabbit to the menagerie. Dave, who a year ago was regularly overruled by Dee, is now in a position to at least demand a compromise: no new rabbit until some of the existing animals have dropped off their running wheels. Way to go, Dave! The other noticeable thing about the living room was the newly acquired dance mat, the family's novelty way of keeping fit while dancing to music. As well as deciding to lose some pounds through regular exercise, Dee has also gone for a more general make-over. A now fluffier, more feminine Dee looks younger and happier as the experience of seeing herself on television was enough to want to 'make something more' of herself.

What is undeniable is that Sonia was the star of the first episode, who's self control and easy good humour made a very strong impression on viewers. This was exactly what she wanted, as she had, according to the show's director, been determined to try to present a positive image for black people, and for black women in particular. She obviously succeeded, and came across as intelligent, fun, and with a lot of common sense, especially when dealing with the Jackson girls. The younger daughter, Carol, became a friend and, in effect, an ally, and the two clearly got on very well; seeing Carol's evident enjoyment at dressing up for an evening out with Sonia was one of the highlights of the episode.

Mary was a tougher nut to crack, but although she put up a fierce resistance to Sonia, it was clear that in terms of trying to throw her off balance, she didn't stand a chance. Sonia's combination of laughter and amused horror at Mary's behaviour was very effective in disarming her. Even now, looking back on it, Sonia is remarkably generous to someone who was extremely rude to her.

As a result, Sonia says, people of all races stopped her in the street after the programme and congratulated her on how well she had handled the situation. Her ambition to be a positive role model for the black community was triumphantly achieved.

Since *Wife Swap*, Sonia has started her own business, a speed dating agency. Given her position as one of the faces of *Wife Swap*, the business idea was bound to be a step in the right direction, and on the update show, we see her with a large group of clients at her first evening of speed dating, supported by Lance.

After the swap, Lance realised how much Sonia meant to him, especially after his experience with Dee, proposed to her in a rose garden – much to her surprise, judging by her response, 'I thought he was having a laugh.' Although Lance learnt a lot from the programme – including that plenty of people disagreed with him, even if he felt that the majority took his side – he remains as determined to be in charge of the family as ever, 'I will have the last word, I will'

So what has Lance learnt? Primarily how lucky he is to have Sonia as his partner. What has Sonia learnt? That she has the confidence and capability to handle most situations.

Another unforgettable episode was the one involving Barry and Michelle, and Carol and Pete. The two couples were as unlike as it is possible to imagine: Barry is a professional gambler, his wife the homemaker, while Pete is a 'modern' husband who helps around the house as well as working, and Carol is a successful career woman.

Carol and Pete went into *Wife Swap* in the hope that it would provide useful publicity for their agency and theatre workshops. 'We have the biggest drama workshop outside London, and one of the biggest in the country' says Carol, a woman with stacks of energy and initiative, and who clearly loves her work.

We got an amazing amount of recognition from people in the industry, and it gave our business a much higher general profile, which is why we had gone into it in the first place. And the other day someone in the industry, and who I hadn't seen for a while, crossed a crowded room shouting, 'It's Carol Godby!' as he'd seen me on the programme.

They found the experience of appearing on *Wife Swap* 'exhausting' and not one either of them would repeat, although a bit of local celebrity goes a long way. Pete found himself being asked to autograph the arms of a group of young lads with the words 'Pete from Wife Swap' recently, and like many of the swapees still gets recognised by the general public. This can be nice, but it can also be a bit spooky, as Carol explains: 'Someone came up to me the other day and said, "My Mum's a bit eccentric. She likes to spot famous people, and then just follow them around. She followed you all round Tesco's last week!"' Celebrity status is one thing, but attracting a stalker is quite clearly another, less predictable, side effect of *Wife Swap*!

Carol had to cope with Barry, the professional gambler who, according to his wife Michelle, hadn't made her a cup of tea in 15 years. Carol was at first frightened about meeting him.

Michelle described him in the Household Manual as 'The Lord and Master' and he sounded a bit of an ogre. I was expecting someone much bigger, physically, so when I saw Barry initially it was a bit of a relief – but I soon realised how difficult he could be, though I knew how to handle him.

Barry famously kept shouting her name when he wanted something, generally from the crack of dawn and most likely involving porridge. His cries of 'Carol! Carol!' made him a star, but didn't harm her PR campaign either. 'Everyone was copying him after the programme was shown, and on Radio 1 all the disc jockeys seemed to enjoy saying "Carol! ... Carol!" in between playing records. So, by wearing my name out by shouting it so often, he did me a big favour, and I got loads of free publicity and name recognition!'

Carol is still surprised at the extent of Michelle's animosity towards her: 'You actually see and hear her say she'd like to punch me, which is bizarre. I find her a bit frightening really. I decided that there was no way I was going to get involved in a slanging match. I knew she was a jealous woman, so I just said how nice Barry had been to me – and he could be when he wanted to – and that he had made me a cup of tea, which I knew would wind her up – and it did!'

One of the sub-plots of the episode showed Michelle's teenage son, Stephen, getting on very well with Carol, and enjoying her drama workshops, which he still attends.

Carol remains conscious that Pete was shown in a one-sided way as a 'house husband', when, 'In fact he's the other half of our business and works very hard.' Even though she continued to go to work during the shooting of *Wife Swap*, they scrupulously avoided seeing each other in their mutual workplace, as the rules insisted.

To their disappointment, the swap ended less than halfway through, and Carol didn't have her chance to change Barry's house. 'I would have loved to have taken him to the theatre and made a fuss of him. I was going to introduce him to my friends, and he was really looking forward to coming along to one of my workshops, too.' Pete was also sorry the episode ended sooner than expected, though for him it was a bit of a strain, but he is glad to have taken part, explaining;

It reinforced my appreciation of Carol. We were close anyway, but it was good to have a reminder of what she's like – I call her Super Caz as she gets so muc done, she's got so much energy.

Pete and Carol met up with Barry and Michelle some time after their acrimonious last meeting in front of the cameras: 'We wanted some sort of closure on the experience, which we didn't feel we'd had. And Barry and Michelle are both different people when off camera.' This meeting confirmed Pete's belief that Michelle has many, very different moods, musing, 'She seemed like a different person on different days. When she was staying at our house there was a scene where she was filmed having a bubble bath, and she was very concerned, she didn't want her breasts showing, and I thought that was understandable, that she must be a sensitive woman – and then a month or so after *Wife Swap* she went and posed topless for the *Sunday Sport*!'

Carol felt sorry for Stephen: 'He was very upset that his Mum had posed topless. I made sure none of the others in his (drama) group said anything to him about it. It wasn't fair to Stephen for them to have a go at Michelle.' Michelle, for her own part, found the *Wife Swap* experience a very positive one, and revelled in the attention that she and Barry received from the press and the public. They made several television appearances, and became, she feels, 'The King and Queen of *Wife Swap*!'

One thing that hasn't changed is Michelle's attitude towards Carol, which remains one of fairly unremitting hostility. Her connection with Stephen still rankles, though she acknowledges that the *Sunday Sport* pictures caused problems at home: 'He's a bit shy and he got a lot of stick from his friends after the programme and when the pictures came out. But posing topless for a newspaper is something that I always wanted to do. And anyway, people walk about topless on a beach. I'm proud of my body, and I would still have done it, whatever, because I think if you have a dream then you ought to follow it.'

The immediate aftermath of the programme wasn't very good for the Seabournes – they split up over the porridge issue. Happily, they were soon reunited. According to Michelle, this was because Barry, backed down on his demand for daily porridge. According to Barry it happened because Michelle was 'crying like a new-born baby' and he took pity on her and had her back. No change in their differing perspectives on married life there, then!

But had *Wife Swap* changed their lives? Was she a new wife? Was he a new husband? 'Barry has to accept that I'll only make his porridge if I feel like it,' says Michelle. 'That porridge ruined our lives for years.' She is now a much more liberated woman, in that she expects Barry to help look after himself. Barry has to put up with it if he wants Michelle, which he still does. Michelle doesn't expect Barry to completely change, nor does she want him to. Emotionally, she was quite disillusioned during her time away from home: 'I wanted to see what life would be like with what I call a "society husband", by which I mean a man who looks after his wife, treats her nicely, does something for her.'

For Michelle, Pete was just too much of a gent, and she realised that she quite liked having a 'traditional' husband, despite the fact that she wanted to modify his behaviour a bit. Speaking of Pete, she says, 'He said that I was Barry's slave, but I reckon he was – and is – just as much Carol's slave.' Sounds like the fighting spirit is still alive and kicking, but she admits initially that she had liked what she'd seen,

This was a nice family, I was treated well, and I realised that something was very wrong with my life. I sort of knew that anyway, as I was determined to try to see life from a different angle, to live another life, see another side, to have the chance, away from Barry, to explore my thoughts.

She also now admits that she had decided to tell Barry that she was going to leave him when they met to celebrate their third wedding anniversary. It was clear she had done a lot of thinking and talks openly about her disappointment at their wedding day…

Our wedding were a joke. He barely stayed at the reception, and some people thought that the best man was my husband, as he was the one dancing with me most of the evening. My real husband had buggered off. I sort of knew it would be a disaster because Stephen accidentally dropped the wedding cake – a nice traditional one with three tiers – on the floor, and the dog ate half of it, so we had to borrow a plastic one and pretend to cut it. So much for having your cake and eating it!

Romantically, their third anniversary was going to be the moment when Michelle announced she was leaving her husband. Barry, however, with masterly timing, mentioned casually that he loved her.

'I'd been prepared to tell him that I didn't want that life any more,' says Michelle. 'But when he said he loved me I wanted to jump out the car and run about. It were great... I can't describe it.' Barry's confession temporarily saved the marriage, but despite their break up and subsequent reunion (minus the porridge), they faced a further source of friction – a move from their home in Heywood to Southport; a seaside resort about fifty miles away. Michelle never really took to it, and missed her house and her family, so they moved back to Heywood not long after their initial relocation. On reflection, Michelle she thinks that the sight of them rowing, on the update as well as the original programme, could help other people:

'They can see that some other couples row all the time, too, that there's nothing wrong or weird about them, just because they argue a lot. I hope watching us and seeing that I've got the strength to get through things, will give them some strength too.'

What did she think, looking back, about the other *Wife Swap* episodes? 'I would have liked to have been in the first episode. I'd have sorted out Dee's kids, no trouble!' Did it bring her the fame she wanted? 'Yes, we were on the telly... everyone seemed to recognise us. I enjoyed it!' So Michelle has achieved her ambition by getting on television, going topless in a national newspaper and – partially – by reforming Barry.

Finding anywhere in the country where the topic of conversation in the office or down the pub hasn't been *Wife Swap* is a pretty tall order, as the other contributors – Kate and Tracey, Anne and Diane – found out. Having your personal habits broadcast to several million homes is a daunting experience, as Trevor, Kate's husband, discovered, joking;

In the programme Tracey asks me to pull the plug out of the bath when I've finished with it, and afterwards lots of people stopped me in the street and said 'Urgh! Trevor! Can't you pull your own plug out?'

Anne and Diane, who clashed during their *Wife Swap* reunion, found themselves recognised, not only in this country, but internationally. Diane was greeted with 'You were on *Wife Swap*!' when on holiday in Ireland, several months after their episode was shown, while Anne was similarly recognised while in Cuba.

The two women, in many ways the most similar of the contestants remain distant, each thinking the other unreasonable. In Anne's case it is more a case of bearing a grudge against Graham, Diane's husband, while Diane continues to think of Anne as a bossy over-achiever. Both women say that members of the public come up to them to sympathise with them, though both are well aware that people who disagree with them are likely to keep quiet, and that people who know them are more likely to be predisposed to side with them in any case.

For Diane, it was a case of people saying that Anne had a big problem in that she was obsessive about her house, whereas for Anne it was people saying to her, 'How could you stand that man – I'd have given him a slap!' Looking back on her experience, Diane thinks 'I felt I was thrown in at the deep end. I never realised how different and difficult being in someone else's house could be.' The few little criticisms that were made about her clearly still rankle and she claims that her portrayal wasn't sufficiently rounded, 'They showed me how they wanted me to be shown. I do work full time as well as managing the house, but I can do this because I'm more

Both wives appreciate their husbands all the more since the swap: Anne because she had found Graham such a chauvinist, Diane because she thought Rob was a bit too placid for her liking.

flexible than Anne. She comes from a house where writing down lists about everything is "normal".' Doesn't seem that there's much danger of forgiving or forgetting there then…

When she returned to Graham, whom she now affectionately calls 'My little male chauvinist' she says she came back with a fresh outlook; 'Perhaps it was me that was wrong, perhaps my house was too cluttered. When things got a bit untidy I'd think to myself, I wonder what wonder-woman Anne would say if she saw this?'

Perhaps because Graham seemed to come across as such a chauvinist, pointing out 'his mother was very upset by the programme', Diane is quick to defend him, emphasising that his 5am starts every morning left Graham exhausted. When he was filmed watching Anne cook dinner, the man was so tired he could hardly stand up, she points out. Anne remains unmoved by any defence of Graham, but feels that the experience, which did at least give her, as she had wanted, a taste of someone else's life, had a very positive effect on her.

Our family was fairly close anyway, but this brought us that much closer. It made me appreciate Rob more, and for both of us it confirmed that what we've got works.

Perhaps the most dramatic change to any of the wives involved in *Wife Swap* is that of Traccy. A working Mum who took great pride in her career, she swapped with mother of six, Kate. Tracey and Kate had a ferocious fight at the reunion, watched by their bemused husbands. Both admitted the other touched a nerve; with Tracey it was over Kate's accusations of her being an absent mother; with Kate, about not having the most organised or cleanest of houses.

Tracey seemed to take her experience – and Kate's criticisms – to heart. She ditched her gruelling commute, taking a job nearer to home and also became pregnant for the second time in 2003. She now spends far more time with Lottie and she feels much happier being a more hands-on parent.

Tracey's experience was like that of many of the swapees – they wanted to see if life in someone else's shoes would be any better. By and large though, the wives learnt some useful lessons and discovered the grass, as always, is greenest at home. It remains to be seen what the effect will be on the next generation of wives when they unite to tell their stories… we can only wait and see.

5 EXCUSES FOR NOT HAVING MADE THE DINNER...

1. The cooker's on the fritz. I think we might need a new one.

2. I was mugged on the way back from the shops and would you believe it? They took all our fishfingers.

3. I could have sworn you said you were going to be out tonight.

4. I did cook dinner. You ate it half an hour ago. These memory lapses of yours are beginning to worry me.

5. Did you not see the news? There was a leaky gas main – if I'd turned on the oven I could have blown up the street.

5 EXCUSES FOR FORGETTING YOUR PARTNERS' BIRTHDAY...

1. Has it really been a year since your last one? Blimey, time does fly when you're so blissfully happy, doesn't it?

2. I thought you didn't want to be reminded you were getting old?

3. I was going to make you a present, but there's still washing-up liquid in the bottle. I'll pop to the shops tomorrow, but whatever I buy isn't going to be as good as what I planned to make...

4. I couldn't get you what you really wanted, and didn't want to compromise by getting you something that's second best. So, I suppose you'd better give me a list, then...

5. That bloody website, they said it would be delivered today. I'll chase them up on that, don't you worry. I'm sure it'll be with you tomorrow. Shall I get you a cuppa in the meantime?

The Stresses and Strains of Famin' it

WIFE SWAP

Reality TV shows like *Wife Swap* rely on members of the public baring their souls before several million people, and they must know (especially anyone taking part in the second series) that the more conflict there is on screen the more exciting the programme is to watch.

So doesn't this mean that they're bound to be set up for a fall? Or is that a knee-jerk reaction to programmes that actually have a positive effect? Can the lure of fame be an over-riding impulse that nothing can get in the way of?

Andy Warhol, the 1960s artist and film-maker, earned his own immortality by coming up with one of the most-quoted sayings of the late twentieth-century. Speaking of the television culture that was already beginning to dominate the Western world, he said 'In the future everybody will be world famous for fifteen minutes.' Most people drop the 'world' part when they quote him, which makes his quip even more applicable, to our domestic television shows.

Appearing on a reality TV programme is certainly one of the quickest ways to fame, and the cult of this type of celebrity came full circle in *Wife Swap* when Jade Goody, who became famous by appearing on *Big Brother*, took part in the *Celebrity Wife Swap* episode. She and her partner Jeff, swapped with Major Charles Ingram and his wife Diana, both of whom had also become famous through the television quiz show *Who Wants To Be A Millionaire?*

We know that reality TV is popular, and that *Wife Swap* was the smash hit of 2003, with viewing figures comfortably above five million and rave reviews in newspapers and magazines. What makes it so popular is the way we see into other people's lives, watch their deepest neuroses come out, and see them criticised on their most sensitive points by complete strangers. What's not to like?

A number of the media comments referred to the programmes as 'car crash' TV, and there seems to be a prejudice that says that taking part in such programmes, especially those with the more confrontational moments, is deeply damaging to individuals. But, although some shouting matches can be pretty cringe-inducing –

and there have been some pretty spectacular bust-ups on the show – the point about *Wife Swap* is that it is an overwhelmingly positive series, albeit one that's comparable with tackling an assault course: it isn't always pretty, there's a lot of effort involved, people get mucky... but at the end of it they come out more confident and having learned something about themselves by being put through a few life-changing experiences.

As we see in the *Swappers United* section of this book, the couples who took part in series one of *Wife Swap* all found that their partnerships were strengthened by the experience, and that they appreciated their other halves that much more after having experienced what it was like to live (and only for 10 days!) with someone else in their house. Even if there were some temporary blips in their relationship, they have overcome the stresses and strains of not just being under scrutiny by a camera crew, but also having their lifestyle and values called into question by the great British public as well. Certainly, the couples who took part in the first series not only learnt this, but also became famous in the process.

Interestingly, it was the more combative couples who became best known. This may justify the comment that people like to watch conflict – or it's probably fair to say that those who shout loudest, get heard! The larger-than-life antics of some of the couples tended to make more of a splash in reviews and got us all talking about them around that famous 'water-cooler' we congregate around.

The argument against reality TV programmes is that they put people under a great deal of psychological and emotional stress, but for example in Barry and Michelle's case the conflict was essentially between the two of them, even when they weren't in the same house! As the update episode proved, they don't need to be put into other people's homes to actually enjoy a massive row.

Let's face it, any relationship that can keep up a war of attrition over making breakfast year in, year out, has to at least partly function because of conflict, let alone despite it!

The most spectacular example of stress is arguably Lizzie's jealousy of having Emma in her house, in series two. It could be argued that someone so acutely worried about the potential threat from having another woman in her house should probably have given more thought to taking part in the first place. It could also be said that this was perhaps a case of the desire for fame overriding common sense and caution.

But, equally, it could also be argued that the episode actually proves that it's only when we are placed in unusual or stressful situations like those in *Wife Swap* that the important issues in our lives break through the surface and have to be confronted, for better or worse.

It's like getting that sense of satisfaction from picking a particularly aggravating spot. As Lizzie herself says in her episode, after she'd spoken her mind to Colin, she felt much better about having got various issues off her chest. That'll do it every time. Effectively, it is only by putting yourself in these situations that you can identify and deal with these issues. And if taking part in stressful activities should be frowned on, let alone actively discouraged, then no one would ever go on holiday, move house, have children, change jobs, try to set the timer on the video... If your life settles into a mundane routine, is that healthy in itself? Shouldn't we try and look for some challenges in our lives? The trouble is, how do you know whether your routine is normal, reasonable or even right for you, unless you try another one?

This, as much as a desire to 'be on the telly', is why the various families who have taken part in both series of *Wife Swap* found themselves in our front rooms in the first place. The wives in particular were to be thrown in at the deep end, literally packing their bags and leaving home for nearly two weeks to try this different life. However nervous they were in doing this, they were also looking forward to it: it was the point of their taking part. As the Ingrams say in the celebrity episode, it may look like divorce, with the wife packing everything in a determined manner and moving out, but 'divorce doesn't feel this jolly'.

'Jolly' may not be the word that springs to mind when watching the various reunions at the end of each episode. When Michelle tells Carol that if she's no good at housework then she's failed as a woman, or when Kate and Tracey trade insults over the way they bring up their children, it may well make the viewers squirm from the safety of their sitting-room. But ironically, the end result of each episode has been an upbeat one. Not so much a car crash, then, as a lifeboat. There may have been lots of waves, the contributors were often emotionally battered and bruised, but they were brought safely to shore and though the ride was bumpy they had at least emerged from a voyage with a new sense of themselves – oh, and they were famous, and for a lot longer than Warhol's fifteen minutes.

The Six Most Common
Relationship Sticking Points

1. YOU EXPECT DIFFERENT THINGS

Everyone has a different set of assumptions on how everyday life should properly function. From the basics of what food you cook, to how often you clean the oven, we all go into relationships from varying family backgrounds, with entirely different systems of routines and values. While one partner won't see the need to set foot in a church again after they tie the knot, for the other it's a rule to go to mass once a day and twice on Sundays. Herein lies a problem.

TIP: Bear in mind that everyone is different, compare your relationship and its domestic day with your friends' and see how it varies from your own. Nobody's perfect, but once you're settled, keep working at those communication skills to stay on track.

2. YOU DON'T COMMUNICATE

If you spend all day at work phoning / faxing / emailing, by the time you go home, your conversational levels can be reduced to 'What's for dinner' and 'When does the football start?' The daily grind wears us all down, but it's essential to make time to talk to your partner if you're feeling fed up or stuck in a rut. If you are constantly veering from monotony into rows, it's about time to set aside a couple of hours a week to raise issues, discuss them and make your partner feel appreciated or make them understand why you don't.

TIP: Don't get complacent, basic manners and a few 'thank you's can make the world of difference. Try not to be too quick to judge or snap at the slightest provocation, but make an effort to think about your partner and what he or she needs and responds to.

3. ONE OF YOU WANTS MORE SEX

The lights go off and one of you is sound asleep, while the other one is a frustrated bundle of sexual tension. Not a good way to get through the week. Once a sexual issue is raised, it either turns into a real bone of contention or gets ignored until a cursory encounter puts it back in the box until next time. It's not unusual to have different libido levels in a relationship, but you can find a balance if you are prepared to tackle the situation.

TIP: Be honest: if you find it difficult to communicate verbally, write your partner a letter. Explain why you can't always be ready for sex and try to resolve any other factors that may come into play, such as tiredness, stress or lack of privacy.

4. THERE'S MESS EVERYWHERE AND IT'S DRIVING YOU MAD

An odd sock lying around shouldn't lead to too much pain and suffering, but if you've asked for it to be put away every day since the Battle of Waterloo, sooner or later, someone's going to end up in Casualty. The home environment should be a relaxing place, so try not to let it turn into a battleground for the want of a few basic household rules that everyone can follow.

TIP: Explain why you find the clutter or mess hard to deal with and try to work out a sensible compromise with the other members of your household. You can each have a drawer where you throw all your odds and sods in a haphazard fashion, but don't let it extend all over the house!

5. MONEY, MONEY, MONEY...

If you thought rowing about that odd sock was a strain, getting your knickers in a twist about money is going to get your blood pressure rising like nothing else. Your partner might think it's perfectly acceptable to spend the housekeeping money at the pub, but if you know that your next take-away is going to be funded by an HP scheme on 29 per cent interest, you've got every right to raise the matter. And if you're having the same discussion on a regular basis, it's definitely time to review your finances and make some realistic decisions.

TIP: Don't be lured into arguments that pick over every purchase on a daily basis. Put aside some time to set sensible budgets for essentials, luxuries and emergency funds for unexpected bills. Review your plans regularly and it'll be much less scary when the bank statement arrives.

6. ROWS, ARGUMENTS, BUST-UPS

Everybody needs someone to spark off and a relationship that doesn't experience a cross word from time to time is going to fizzle out faster than a damp firework. But every day is too often for conflict, so if you are feeling like there's a row brewing, take a few minutes to work out a strategy and decide what you want the end result of your bust-up to be. From just clearing the air to finding a remedy for a major problem, don't start your rant until you know you can control when to stop. Do your best to choose a time and place when you can say your piece in private: arguing when out in public or with friends/kids/family is not going to make for a happy ending and washing your dirty linen in public is not a good look.

TIP: Take a time-out if your row is getting too heated or if you are liable to end it by sulking or saying things you'll later regret. Have a breather and return to the matter when you've both had time to consider it and have thought about how to work through the problem together.

WIFE SWAP DO'S AND DONT'S.

Tips for Wives

Do adapt to your new household routine with grace and serenity.

Don't say 'bollocks to the children' and give up.

Do try to be patient and respectful of your new husband's opinions.

Don't call him 'an arrogant piece of shit in shoes'.

Do leave your new household having gained a greater comprehension of family dynamics.

Don't leave your shoes behind in the rush to get away.

Do cook tasty and nutritious meals for your new family.

Don't do it all three hours too early so that it's cold by the time everyone's ready to eat.

Do do your share of the housework.

Don't sit in a chair, gathering moss, staring into space for hours.

WIFE SWAP DO'S AND DONT'S.

Tips for Families

Do work to create a harmonious environment by following your new Mum's rules.

Don't call her a 'fat f***ing slag' and slam the door in her face.

Do try and follow her dinner rota.

Don't order a take-away and hide the leftovers in the cupboard when she gets home.

Do pull your weight around the house.

Don't sit there for hours on end, shouting your new partner's name in the vague hope that she'll come and attend to you.

Do keep an open mind about your new partner's cooking.

Don't ask your kids 'have you spat it out yet?' before you've even tried it yourself.

Do play quietly and responsibly.

Don't laugh at your new Mum as she gets more and more frustrated and angry.

WIFE SWAP

Celebrity Wife Swap

The Couples

Charles and Diana Ingram have been together for twenty years and have three daughters. They achieved celebrity status thanks to appearing on the quiz show *Who Wants To be A Millionaire*. The couple say they are 'each other's rock' and are a close family unit with their three daughters.

Pregnant Jade Goody and her partner Jeff Brazier are around 15 years younger than the Ingrams. Jade became a household name after taking part in *Big Brother* in 2002, while Jeff is a television presenter. The couple have a stormy relationship, punctuated by screaming matches, which Jeff puts down to Jade going through a tough pregnancy and comments wryly,

To say Jade's hormonal is an understatement… believe me, I get it!

Name: Jeff Brazier
Age: 24
Occupation: TV Presenter

Before Jade leaves for the swap, however, they look very much in love and Jeff reassures her, 'I'm going to miss you very, very much.'

While Jeff and Jade share a modern flat in a new development in Essex, the Ingrams live in a large Georgian house in Wiltshire. They have a traditional household with a structured routine; Diana takes care of the daily chores and tasks, while Charles 'looks after the bigger issues'. This will be the first time that Diana has spent more than a couple of days away from the girls, but Charles is more concerned that he'll 'miss sex' so reveals he 'had a top-up last night', much to his wife's embarrassment. Sometimes, you can just have too much information…

Unlike the other couples in the *Wife Swap* series, the celeb couples have been given a clue as to where they are going. Diana has been told that she will swap with Jade, while Jade knows that a swap with the Ingrams is a possibility. Although Diana and Charles haven't watched the programme, they have heard of *Big Brother* and realise they will be swapping with a much younger couple. Diana states her concerns as:

My biggest fear is having to sit in a nightclub most nights until 4am.

Name: Jade Goody
Age: **22**   Status: **Partners**
Occupation: **TV Celebrity**
Location: **Essex**
Children: **Bobby Jack (0)**

Charles is looking forward to taking this feisty filly in hand and to showing her who's boss, declaring, 'I think she needs to be dominated a bit.' Steady on, Charles, it's not that kind of show…

Similarly, Jade has her reservations about the possibility of staying at the Ingrams'. As she is driven deeper into the countryside, she realises it's the well-to-do Ingrams' home she's approaching and decides 'They won't like me!' Time can only tell…

Arriving

Once she reaches the house and has done battle with the garden gate, Jade has a good look around the house, and gives the wedding photographs of Diana and Charles the once-over. She also decides after going around the comfortable family home that, 'They must have a bit of money,' but her worst nightmare is confirmed when she reaches the kitchen and clocks the electric hob – not something that she thinks she can cook on. Will the Ingram family be

Name: **Charles Ingram**
Age: **39**
Occupation: **Ex-Army Officer**

on a salad-only diet if Jade can't get the cooker to work? Will Charles lower his standards and get to grips with the smaller issues and help her to turn the hob on?

By contrast, Diana finds her new home rather bleak: 'Oh my God, no curtains! Isn't that strange?' She notices the prominent position that the television has in the flat: it's clearly going to be an issue between her and Jeff, and she doesn't really approve of too much telly. She also raises her eyebrows at the contents of the kitchen cupboards, sifting through gravy granules, crisps and squash. She looks positively horrified at the tomato ketchup – perhaps it's an ingredient that doesn't get utilised in the Ingram kitchen too often…

The women then read each other's Household Manual's and Jade is unimpressed at how much Diana seems to do for her husband:

He likes to be waited on hand and foot? Well, Charles, I'll cook you a good dinner and that'll be it.

Name: Diana Ingram
Age: **39**   Status: **Married**
Occupation: **Housewife**
Location: **Wiltshire**
Children: **Portia (13), Rosie (11), Hester (8)**

The first job to get in hand, however, is cooking the children's dinner, so Jade sets to work with a pan of spuds and tackles that tricky hob straight on. So far, so good…

Over at the flat, Diana is recovering from the food cupboard reconnaissance and is checking the routine in Jeff's home. Will her new Essex lifestyle be a bit of a culture shock or sow the seeds of a revolution on her return to Wiltshire?

Meet The Family

The initial introductions go very smoothly. Charles forms a good opinion of Jade straight away, telling his video diary, 'My immediate impression? She's a really nice girl.' He also makes the observation, 'Jade seems to interact with the children far better than I do,' having seen how warmly she greets his daughters with an ice-breaking hug and kiss. Charles offers to make dinner for his new wife on her first night, but seems a bit, erm, confused by the kitchen. Digging about for some parmesan, he is soon keeping up a stream of consciousness from within the fridge, including the telling phrase, 'You can tell I don't often go in here!' We're guessing food shopping probably doesn't fit within the remit of dealing with 'big issues'…

Being a friendly kind of guy, Jeff does his best to make Diana welcome, but his questions about her age seem to annoy her somewhat. On learning she's 39, he laughs, 'Thirty-nine? That's the same age as my mum!' Diane's not amused. Jeff, you're doing yourself no favours, mate! Jeff then confirms one of Diana's many fears by keeping the television on, with the volume cranked up, the whole time. She's less than impressed and states,

I find the television being on the whole time quite hard… in my house there are plenty of other things to do.

Looks like our boy is going to get a bit of a shock when the tables are turned. Jeff is also amused when Diane reveals that her husband likes to have a bit of a chat, 'Charles doesn't stop talking,' repeating emphatically, 'He doesn't stop!'

What are the 'big issues' that stop your man sharing the housework?!

Getting To Know You...

Jeff decides to get out of the flat and take Diana, a country girl at heart, to his weekly round of golf. Acting as his caddy, she tries to participate, but isn't enjoying herself and Jeff is worried about her inability to relax, 'She was as stiff as a board. I'd like to beat her down a little bit.' Diana admits that her image isn't a very approachable one, and that she can seem a bit off-putting: 'I've got a hard image, I've been referred to as "hatchet-faced" and some people seem to think that I'm not really human.'

At the Ingrams', Jade seems to have settled in and is pottering around the kitchen, making the packed lunches, and proving the point that when it comes to Marmite, you really do either love it or hate it. The expression on her face as she scrapes the filling onto the bread is priceless, along with the revelation 'I have never made a Marmite sandwich before.' Thank goodness this historic revelation is caught on camera! Charles explains to Jade that he and Diana work as a team around the house, 'We do it together, really... it's teamwork.' Jade doesn't agree, and thinks there are far more things

Dancing isn't just about co-ordination… get your 'bling' working and your dancing shoes on to lose your inhibitions!

that Diana does than he is even aware of. Mopping the floor, doing the laundry and all the cooking would be a struggle for most women, but at seven months pregnant, an exhausted and exasperated Jade looks like a woman on the verge of a nervous breakdown when she announces, 'If I have a premature baby, I'm blaming it on the Ingrams. Overworked and underpaid!'

She soon puts her foot in it when she accuses Charles of flapping. After a career in the Army this is deeply insulting, and Charles' comment, 'What she said was very annoying, very ill-considered,' shows that he isn't a happy chappy. In a slightly petulant tone, he says, 'I think I'm a remarkably composed person.' Oops, Jade really touched a nerve there!

Thankfully, Jade passes the next of her wifely tests – cooking a large Sunday lunch – with flying colours. Flapping aside, Charles does his bit in preparation for their guests' arrival. From cutting a dash in wellies as he mows the lawn, to darting about laying the table, he gets the jobs done in ship-shape fashion, although his multiple fly-past's in the kitchen keep Jade's eyes rolling in their sockets. 'What a palaver,' she comments pithily. It all turns out well, though, and once everyone is seated, Charles kindly thanks Jade for her hard work with a hug and a kiss. Aah, domestic bliss rules – for the moment at least…

Diana has also been hit – again – on one of her more sensitive buttons, complaining to her video diary,

I've lost count of the times Jeff refers to my age. I'm beginning to feel that I'm ready for the scrap heap.

For his part, Jeff is concerned that Diana is still too stiff and uncomfortable, and decides that what she needs is a night out on the town at one of the nightclubs that she actually dreads going to. Ever the gentleman, he buys her a trendy outfit to go clubbing in, and introduces some 'bling' into her Wiltshire wardrobe with new jeans, jacket and a natty hat. As he whips the new clothes out of the bag with the enthusiasm of a magician pulling a rabbit out of a hat, he asks, 'Jacket – are you feeling that?' Diana just looks somewhat bemused at this new turn of phrase and probably wonders if she's being asked to identify the fibres in its weave. Seeing her doubtful expression, he tells her, 'You're going to be throwing moves you never thought possible!' Crikey, a nation awaits with baited breath to see if Diana will become the new Kylie. Unfortunately, and even when he means well, he can't leave the age issue alone, telling her once she's in her outfit, 'Mrs Ingram, you are busting that out. Do you think you look younger?' 'Until I met you, Jeff, I didn't feel that old,' responds Diana, wearily.

The new-look Diana really isn't looking forward to the evening out, especially the dancing part. 'The only time I went to an aerobics class I was sent straight to the back as my co-ordination was so bad!' she muses. But the night out turns out to be a brilliant idea. Jeff primes his mates to make sure she enjoys herself, telling them they need to 'get a little bit of a drink down her' – he is determined she will relax and enjoy herself. After starting the evening by looking extremely nervous, Diana finds Jeff's friends 'really nice' and after a few drinks and some encouragement, she loosens up. After 'bustin' out' some moves on the dance floor, Diana genuinely appears to be letting her hair down and, in the process, looks several years younger! Reaching home she confides, 'I did enjoy it. Jeff is very kind and considerate, and the evening was not as bad as I was expecting.' Phew!

Back at the Ingrams', poor old Jade is feeling a bit down in the dumps and has a little weep in front of the video diary, tearfully describing how much she is missing Jeff. It's obvious that she is really starting to get fed up with all the chores, so Charles had better watch his step once her rules come into play...

Turning The Tables

Although she and Jeff are now on much more relaxed terms, Diana shows no mercy when it comes to implementing her rules in the house. Television is banned, with Diana explaining that in her house, time is spent more constructively, doing interesting things. Jeff's not convinced, but does get his nose stuck into a book on dogs that Diana has bought him. The reading is because she wants to introduce him to her world, which will mean several new experiences, one of which is buying a new pet. The Ingrams already have a large dog (called Simba) at home, and Charles has banned having any more, but Diana buys a small terrier to take home. Meanwhile the little dog completes the new, temporary family she has set up with Jeff. This also provides one of their funnier moments when Jeff asks her about bitches, and how easy it is to stop pet dogs from getting pregnant. When Diana says 'In certain cases dogs try quite hard to get to a bitch' Jeff throws back, 'Yes, I've got a lot of friends like that!' causing the 'hatchet-faced' woman to crease up with laughter.

Eager to introduce him to some new experiences, Diana buys some sherry, which Jeff, very much an Essex boy and proud of it, hasn't tasted before. 'You're trying to put a little bit of culture into my small-minded Essex brain. Are you supposed to swig it down?' he asks. It's not his cup of tea, but at least he's tried it. While Diana hands out her instructions about the new rules, Jeff touches on the delicate issue of her age again. This gives Diana the opportunity she's been waiting for and she tells him that she wants him to stop referring to it. Jeff is genuinely surprised and hopes he hasn't upset her, but then puts his foot in it again with another reference to his mother: 'After all, 39 isn't that old... my Mum's 39.' Please Jeff... put a sock in it.

Back at the Ingrams' house, Jade thinks that Diana is expected to do too much on her own. When it comes to setting her own rules she triumphantly tells an astonished Charles, 'From now all that Diana is supposed to do – you do!' and hands over the Household Manual with a satisfied flourish. She also thinks he needs to spend more time doing fun things with his daughters, like bouncing on the trampoline in the garden. The division of household duties is the one thing that really causes conflict between Jade and Charles, and at one point they have a furious row in the kitchen. Charles argues that she is being completely unfair expecting him to do so much. Jade points to the Household Manual as irrefutable proof that she hasn't asked Charles to do anything more than he expects her or Diana to do, so what's the problem? If she can manage it all at seven months pregnant, then why can't he? Talk about mutiny in the ranks!

The Major is positively incandescent at the thought of being put-down in such a way, and between his shocked dismay and Jade's yelling, it makes for an ear-splitting argument. He accuses her of exaggerating the amount of help she gives Jeff around the house – given she doesn't seem willing to share any of the burdens with him. Jade is unimpressed:

I did Diana's work for days… you've only done one day's worth and already you can't cope!

He really doesn't seem to want to let it lie and is still up in arms about the whole situation when he speaks to his video diary, 'She thinks that Diana and I don't work together very well – which is a bit rich, really, as she's given me the vast amount of jobs to do.' Jade then has a nice relaxing time, chilling out with the Ingram girls and generally leaving Charles to tackle the household chores. Eventually, he does have the good grace to admit, 'This is why Diana's so fit… all this housekeeping'.

The row seems to have cleared the air, though, and in a mirror image of Jeff's makeover with Diana, Jade thinks her temporary husband would be improved by a younger, trendier image.

If tracksuit bottoms are good enough for David Beckham they're good enough for you,

she tells him, marching Charles into a sports shop. A few quick changes later, and the Major has a new hooded top and tracksuit bottoms for relaxing in at home, and is seen striding down the street with his celebrity stylist, wearing a chic pair of shades. Watch out Wiltshire, it's not just Diana who's working her 'bling' now!

On their last evening together, Charles cooks a slap up meal for his stand-in wife and Jade rounds off her evening with the family by getting them to play a board game together. He admits that the big bust-up over the housework helped him realise that Jade's more relaxed way of going about things could make the daily routine less regimented, while she is impressed that he stood up to her. Mutual respect abounds.

Taking some time to do things you wouldn't normally do can stimulate a relationship: get out of the house and visit that exhibition or jump on a trampoline – you might enjoy it!

Diana, meanwhile, is still getting on famously with Jeff. Towards the end of the swap, Jeff asks her advice – as an older woman – about relationships. He confesses Jade and he have terrible rows, and that he wishes someone else could be on the receiving end of her tongue: 'I ask other blokes if they get grief from their missus and some say "Yes", but some say "No" and that ain't fair.' Diana agrees that lots of rows are bad for a relationship, even though they can clear the air, but Jeff wishes that he and Jade could be as secure and relaxed as Diana seems to be when discussing her relationship with Charles.

For their final outing, Diana takes Jeff to the National Gallery in London. 'So what's in here then?' he asks. On the way around, Jeff is really awestruck by the scale of some of the art, 'That's as big as the front of my house!' and declares one of the subjects of a painting, 'Minging'. Diana admits she doesn't have a clue what this means, but once Jeff has explained it means 'unattractive', she still can't bring herself to use it, convinced it's a swear word. The swap ends with a learning experience all around, but the reunion is still to come…

Taking Stock

At the reunion there's rather more tension than expected. This is partly because each couple, once reunited in a hotel room, gets to see a video that the stand-in wife has made. Interestingly, both the Ingram's have worn their new outfits, but while Charles seems impressed with Diana's new look, he certainly wasn't expecting the puppy she bought with Jeff. Jade is shocked to hear Jeff defend Diana's comments about their home and is positively up in arms at the thought of this woman coming into her flat and being so critical, looking more and more astonished as she hears Diana talk about their lack of routine, finally spitting out angrily, 'She's a snob.'

As a result, when they all meet at the reunion, the initial reaction from Jade is one of disgusted silence. Diana partially backtracks as they have a stilted conversation, saying that she probably comes across as rather arrogant and aloof but that in reality she isn't, claiming 'I don't project myself well.' Jade looks particularly unimpressed as once again Jeff defends Diana and a row erupts before they have

If 'sorry' seems to be the hardest word, are you rowing too much?

even left the room. Poor old Jeff gets into even more trouble by suggesting that Diana has broadened his cultural horizons with classical music and art. He ends up having to stick up for himself, telling Jade how typical her over-the-top reaction is. The Major says he has learnt that it would be a good idea 'to be a little more instant', but his wife immediately argues this point, telling him such an idea is totally impractical: plans have to be made, other people need to be considered. Oh, dear, and it was all going so well.

Back at home, neither couple have spontaneously fallen back into the way they acted before their time apart. After the reunion, Charles is very affectionate with Diana, who has to be coaxed into repaying his compliments, while Jade and Jeff aren't on speaking terms. After a long silence, Jade cuddles up to Jeff and apologises. And so, for the moment, everything ends happily, but it remains to be seen if the Ingrams will be going clubbing and Jade and Jeff will be drinking sherry anytime soon...

THE URBAN LIFESTYLE GUIDE TO THE COUNTRY SET MAKEOVER

Follow these handy tips and you too could end up with a pop star wife and a millionaire lifestyle...

FOR HER:

Chuck out that chintz and get yourself a cool tailored jacket and funky bootleg jeans. You can still walk the dogs and look stylish by day in this ensemble and accessorise in the evenings with a belt, tight t-shirt and hat for big-town chic in the Home Counties!

FOR HIM:

Bin that Barbour and wave goodbye to those wellies. The casual man around town can relax just as well in tracksuit bottoms and trainers. And you can now potter around your country pile looking like you're straight out of the hood in the right kind of sweatshirt – like Jade says, 'If it's good enough for David Beckham...'

CELEBRITY WIFE SWAP DRINKING GAME

Take a shot every time you hear...
'MINGING' OR 'I DON'T FLAP!'

Household Manual

Charles & Diana Ingram

How often do you clean your home?
I do a bit every day. Often have a blitz when friends are coming over.

Who does the cleaning in general?
Is this done voluntarily, or only when asked?
I do most voluntarily. Charles helps if I ask/harass him.

Who does the following, and how often...
Hoovering?
I do it every day downstairs.

Dusting?
I do it once a week.

Tidying?
I do most, Charles does some.

Ironing?
I do it twice a week, often on a Sunday night.

Cleaning the bathroom?
I do it about twice a week. Charles has never cleaned the bathroom.

Clothes washing?
I do a load a day, if necessary.

Cleaning the kitchen?
I wipe round every day, wash floor twice a week. Charles does a deep clean on the oven periodically.

Loading the dishwasher (if applicable)?
Everyone loads the dishwasher.

Cleaning the car?
Charles does it once a fortnight.

Gardening?

I do the plants, Charles does mowing and heavy work.

DIY?

Charles does it when required.

Other / what?

Guinea pigs – I help/supervise the girls.

Budgie – the kids do it, but I check it has been done.

Dog – I feed him am and pm and walk him in the morning and afternoon.

Cats – I feed them am and pm

How often do you sit down and eat together?

Saturday and Sunday for three meals and in the week if possible
(schedules permitting).

Where do you eat?

In the dining room.

Who prepares breakfast / lunch / dinner?

I prepare all meals, except for weekday breakfast when everyone sorts out
their own cereal.

Who cooks and when?

I do all the cooking. It's always a proper cooked breakfast at the weekends,
roast chicken on Sunday and sometimes in the week too.

What are your top three dinners?

Roast chicken, spaghetti bolognaise, pizza

Who does the shopping for food and household goods?

I do all the shopping.

How often do you go food / household goods shopping?

Three times a week.

FANTASY CELEBRITY WIFE SWAP!

1. The Beckhams meet the Windsors

Who's the poshest? Victoria learns that there are levels of attention and servility that even she hasn't experienced, but feels a little short-changed by her new husband Philip. David and Elizabeth, meanwhile, get on like a house on fire, and bond over a game of keepy-uppy.

2. Brad Pitt and Jennifer Aniston meet *Big Brother*'s Helen & Paul

Helen thinks new husband Brad is 'lush', but as far as boyfriend Paul is concerned, that is 'so' not cool. Attentive viewers have noticed, however, that Paul keeps trying to engage Jennifer in conversations about "stuff".

3. The Osbournes meet The Simpsons

Sharon steps into her new two-dimensional house to see Bart and Lisa at each other's throats and finds it wearyingly familiar. Marge, meanwhile, moves in with Ozzy and finds him refreshingly alert and articulate compared to Homer.

5 EXCUSES FOR HAVING OVERSPENT ON THE HOUSEHOLD BUDGET...

1. With these new trainers I'll be up and down the stairs with the Hoover that much quicker.

2. You said you wanted to go on a diet anyway. Well, now you have to.

3. If I've learned anything about life from Monopoly it's that we may be broke today, but tomorrow either one of us could win £10 in a beauty contest.

4. It may have cost a few bob, but a new TV is something we can both enjoy.

5. I was putting the money towards a surprise party for you actually, but you've spoiled it now.

WIFE SWAP

The Couples

Jason and Nicola live in a five bedroom mansion in Wales and have two young children, Lewis and Morgan. Jason is a high earner, working in financial services. When he gets home after a hard day's work, he likes to shut himself away in his games room, where he will play on his Playstation for up to four hours at a time. 'I've no involvement in the rest of the house,' he says. 'I've got everything I need here.' Nicola is a freelance interior designer, and has created a beautiful home full of personal touches, 'I've done this all myself,' she says proudly, 'with no help from Jason.' She describes herself as an 'unpaid slave'.

Jason disagrees – she's a paid slave! 'Nic gets paid for everything,' he says, patting her knee. 'And I mean, everything!' Jason spends very little time with the children, generally any family outings tend to take place without him. Lewis is upset at his Dad's lack of interest in him and his general unsociability:

Sometimes he locks himself in his room. I think that's really weird.

Name: **Jason McLoughlin**
Age: **32**
Occupation: **Financial Services**

The one thing that Jason and Nic do have in common is their love of money, 'We like to spend money' she says, and money seems to be the cement that keeps their relationship together.

David and Jayne live in Newcastle and have two children, Lianna and Reece. They work in a canteen and a charity shop respectively. 'Family is the most important thing to us, it's more important that money or worldly goods,' says Dave. 'Children should be the most important thing in your life.' Dave describes himself as a 'new man', and, unlike Jason, he seems to do the vast majority of jobs around the house. His wife Jayne, watching him from the kitchen table, agrees,

I'm not lazy, but I'm not a workaholic.

Arriving

As the wives travel to each other's homes, we're let into a secret: they're sisters-in-law! The two wives have never been close, haven't met each other for nine years, and neither know the other's children. Their husbands are brothers who talk on the phone, but don't meet often.

Name: Nicola O'Sullivan
Age: **32** Status: **Partner**
Occupation: **Interior Designer**
Location: **Bridgend**
Children: **Lewis (7), Morgan (2)**

When they arrive at each other's house, they are still unaware of whose home it is. Jayne is pleased at what she finds – a large and well-decorated mansion – 'Better than I thought!' Nicola arrives at a much smaller house, which isn't as well equipped as hers. The first thing she notices is the smell of cigarette smoke in the living room – 'You should never smoke in your lounge; it's your best room!' Reading the Household Manual, she realises that Dave does all the work, 'He does all the cooking! Wicked!'

Both wives have been left an envelope containing the week's spending money. Jayne is amazed at how much there is: Nicola can't believe how little: after all, she spends about £500 a week on her own family. The idea of coping with a budget of about £40 for food for a whole week seems like an impossible task.

Meet The Family

The real shock, for both women, comes when the men and their children walk through the door, and they realise they've wife swapped with their brother-in-law. The men think it's a great joke, and wonder how their wives are going to get on. Given that Nic does

Name: Dave McLoughlin
Age: 42
Occupation: Catering Industry

most of the work at home, Jason reckons his brother Dave has got the best end of the deal – not very flattering for Jayne. Dave, who does all the housework anyway, thinks the swap's going to be fun, and, knowing how hard Nic works at home, says to the kids, 'Haven't we done well? This is going to be great!'

Getting To Know You...

It's clear from the start that Dave and Nic are going to get on well: they're both warm and outgoing, and used to looking after other people. Nic is amazed at how much Dave does. As well as managing to be a 'new man' in terms of the housework, he's a very affectionate father who spends a lot of time with the children, whether getting them out of or putting them to bed, or playing with them in the back yard.

Dave's family, though they have very little money to speak of, have an outing to the local arcade each weekend, where they play on

Name: **Jayne McLoughlin**
Age: **37** Status: **Married**
Occupation: **Retail**
Location: **Tyne and Wear**
Children: **Reece (9), Lianna (7)**

machines, using two pence pieces that Dave has saved during the week. Although Dave is initially annoyed at Nic's criticism of how basic his kitchen is, and is thrown when, instead of buying some bin bags and gravy, as requested, she actually blows much of the week's budget in a single shopping trip, saying 'I might not find it so funny come Saturday or Sunday when I've nothing to eat,' the two of them get on very well.

This can't be said of Jayne and Jason. He doesn't like the way she irons his shirts, and it is an unusual technique...

Who in their right mind would iron a shirt and then fold it on a bed?

Jayne finds Jason arrogant and unhelpful, and isn't impressed by his argument that he works long hours so shouldn't be expected to help around the house. Things aren't helped when she refuses to be bribed to carry out favours for Jason in the way that Nicola would, even when he offers her £30 to go and buy him some beer. 'You're mollycoddled,' she tells him, 'and it's all Nicola's fault.'

Use bribery sparingly – it can become an expensive habit!

Nicola finds that Dave is the opposite to his brother, and actually experiencing the difference is an eye-opener for her: 'I feel sorry for him, and I see him as a mirror reflection of me.' She and Dave, having swapped notes, come to the conclusion that they are both walked over by the partners, joking with each other,

We've got two lazy buggers.

As she settles in, Jayne notices that Lewis seems very lonely. She's the one who has to take him to his weekly karate lesson – his father hasn't yet done so. Jason meanwhile goes down to the pub, where he plays on the fruit machine. 'The only thing I've got to look forward to is coming here,' he says cheerily. Lewis looks forward to his karate lessons, but would love it if his dad took him for once: 'My Mum's the only one who takes me places. Dad doesn't do anything.' When he asks Jayne to make sure that taking him to his sports club is one of the conditions that she'll impose when the time comes for her to impose her rules on the household, she begins to realise just how isolated the boy is. She asks him whether he ever tells his father that he's lonely, and he says yes, but only when he's bored or sad.

'A trouble shared is a trouble halved.' Make time to listen to each other, and your children…

The problem is his father doesn't listen, it's as if Lewis isn't really there. His defence mechanism is deeply upsetting to his Auntie Jayne. In a matter-of-fact way he says, 'I just pretend he doesn't exist'.

Jason seems oblivious of how his son feels and thinks everything's going reasonably well in the wife swap. He's convinced that he and his brother will have nothing to learn from the experience. The only change, he reckons, is that the girls will realise how lucky they each are; one has a husband who does everything for her, the other with a husband who can pay for everything.

At Dave's, Nic isn't particularly looking forward to going back to Jason. Her time with Dave has made her radically rethink her life. The contrast between Dave's evident care and dedication to his children makes an almost unbearable contrast to her home life with Jason, and she breaks down, just thinking of what her children are missing. Jayne, too, decides that she's got to do something: she's upset at Lewis's unhappiness and that he knows his father won't want to take him to karate lessons even if she makes him.

> *It's not good that a child of that age should have to plead with another adult to change his dad. Kids are there to enjoy while you have the chance.*

Turning The Tables

The first thing Jayne does when it's her turn to decide how the house is run, is hire a locksmith to change the lock on Jason's games room. He's appalled, 'What is going on?' he protests moodily. He's not a happy chappy, but decides to give it a go, even though he continues to argue about it with his sister-in-law. Having taken away his bolt-hole, Jayne tells him her next major change – that Jason will get his children up in the morning, and spend a lot more time with them – starting with a family outing. To Lewis's delight she also insists that Jason take him to karate. The other major alteration is that bribery of any sort is outlawed.

At Dave's house, Nicola is making the opposite alteration. Instead of Dave spending his whole time with the children, he is to take Nic out on her own, and thereby make some space for himself and his wife as a couple rather than as just child minders. Dave decides to do this, even though it means him blowing the £50 annual holiday money on an evening out. He thinks she's well worth it. 'She's a

What's your household budget?
Do you spend £500 or £50 in a week
on household essentials? (And no,
girls, that doesn't include shoes!)

breath of fresh air, and I can't help wondering what she's doing with him.' A little merry after their night on the tiles, they return home, put on party hats and, to the video diary, raise their glasses to the 'happy couple' in Wales. Ah, bless.

The happy couple are, of course, anything but, and Jason's temper is getting worse by the hour. Part of the problem is that he simply doesn't realise how much effort is involved in looking after small children. He's never looked after both kids before, let alone got them up in the morning. Jayne's new rules provide a short, sharp – and unwelcome – shock.

Nicola's rules, of course, go in the opposite direction, as she insists that Dave's children help him with the housework. Dave's eyes are also being opened by this new regime at home, 'Yeah, I'm definitely taken for granted.' Turning to Nicola he asks, 'Are you sure you're going home? Please stay!' and to his video diary, he again praises the effect she's had on him, 'It just seems fresher around her.'

The family that plays together, stays together – make time for outings you can all share in.

Jason's first day out with the children proves a disaster. He can't get his daughter's seat attached, and when they do reach the site of the outing – a ruined castle – Lewis falls in the nearby river and hurts himself. They return home early, with Jason in a foul mood. The family outing has lasted for less than an hour. Jayne, watching his bad-tempered return, can see that he's being challenged by more than his son's fall in the river, deciding 'There's a lot going on inside his head.'

Nicola also has a lot going on in her head – most of it negative thoughts about her husband. She says she loves her children, loves where she lives, but can't stand the thought of returning to a man who acts like a bully and doesn't show anything like the affection that Dave shows to his family: 'I don't understand how he's like it,' she say tearfully.

Back in Wales, however, Jason is increasingly aware of how he's gone wrong up till now. He beams with pleasure after the karate class because Lewis was looking at him frequently, and was so evidently pleased to see him. He's obviously been thinking long and hard about the whole issue.

When you buy a dog, you need a dog license, but with kids there's no manual or license. They are yours and you've just got to get on with it.

Speaking of his hard done by wife, he says thoughtfully, 'How Nic does what she does I'll never know.'

Nicola has made her mind up, 'It's time for a change. If nothing comes from this we'll have to split up.' The contrast between the two families continues to be brought sharply into focus with every day that passes. Simple pleasures like sitting with Dave in the back garden in the evening and chatting over a glass of wine, ram home the fact that she spends so little time with Jason. What she doesn't realise is that, luckily for him, he's becoming a very different man as a result of the *Wife Swap* experience, even coming out with a statement that would have been unthinkable a couple of weeks earlier, 'Money's nothing compared with kissing a kiddy goodnight.' Jayne is pleased with her work, 'He's done well, he's quite happy in himself now': but will it be change enough for Nicola?

Taking Stock

It seems that there's more riding on the reunion than with most episodes of *Wife Swap*. Nicola is determined that things won't go back to how they were and expects to have to leave Jason. At the table, Dave tells Jayne that he's going to make some changes at his house too, and that she'll have to give him a lot more help in future. He feels he's been taken advantage of in the past, and wants all that to end.

Nicola tells Jayne and Dave that though they have their problems, they are at least small; she and Jason are going to split up. Jason hasn't been expecting this at all. He has changed radically in the course of just the last five days, living under Jayne's new rules, and is shocked and upset as he realises that Nicola means exactly what she says.

Jason gives the best speech of his life, telling her how he now realises that their life together was built on an entirely wrong foundation, 'I've treated you like an employee, not a partner' and promises that everything will change. He really loves her, and apologises for the last ten years, 'I've been wrong, and I want to put it right.' Nicola can see that he's genuine, 'There are tears in your eyes!' and is prepared to give him another chance, providing he keeps to his promise to make more of an effort: 'I need change in my life.' Happily the episode ends on a positive note and somehow we know that things are going to be OK.

The View From The Sofa

This episode shows reality television in its best form. The *Wife Swap* experience has a profound effect on what was a superficially successful, but actually very unhappy, marriage, with the husband realising his mistake and changing his ways to benefit his whole family.

The fact that two brothers (albeit some ten years apart in age) should have such different lifestyles was fascinating in itself, but that they should be so different in character is all the more remarkable. Jason's mid-life conversion to a kinder, gentler family man suggests that the family traits that Dave showed were there under the surface all the time, it just took the temporary change of life to make them appear. That, of course, is essentially what *Wife Swap* is all about; people preparing to embrace change to see whether it will have any lasting impact on their own lives; seeing if they can learn lessons from others that they can then apply to themselves.

Despite doing so little at home and treating her husband a bit like a doormat, Jayne proved that she had a good heart and was determined to make Jason behave like a better parent. Dave came out of the programme very well, and so did Nicola, but had Jason not seen the light, as it were, this would have been a very bleak show, showing Lewis's misery, and resulting in a marriage break-up. The fact that the programme strengthened the marriage rather than shattered it, proves that this sort of television, as well as providing entertainment for viewers, can be a genuinely positive and life-changing experience for those taking part. It was pretty good from the vantage point of the sofa too...

Nicola O'Sullivan
Interview

At the end of your episode of *Wife Swap* it looked as though Jason was a reformed character, a changed man. Has that lasted?

Yes! In fact, when I first came home it was almost a bit too much, he was so keen to help I found him getting under my feet. My attitude was, 'we can't expect everything to just change after 11 years of being together. Your new self is only two weeks old.' The important thing is not to let things slip back to where they were.

Is he still banned from his games room?

No, and I think it's fair enough that he has a space of his own. He unwinds there when he comes home late from work, and that's OK as long as he isn't in there too long. The trouble was he'd sometimes stay up all night at his computer, or be so late he'd go to sleep downstairs on the sofa. But it isn't all bad – after all, when he's in there he's out of my way when I'm doing things.

Have you seen much of your brother-in-law Dave and his family since the swap?

Not really, no. It's a long way for them to travel from Newcastle to Wales. Jason and Dave still talk about once a week, though. They can't really afford to come down to visit, and they won't take any money to do so. We do text each other sometimes though, to say 'hello'.

How did you feel when you realised that it was your brother-in-law's family you were swapping with?

At first I thought, 'Oh no, it's going to be really boring', but actually it worked out very well. As you'll have seen, I got very upset about things, about the way my life was going, and I think I opened up much more about it. I was able to talk about Jason much more with his brother Dave, than I would ever have felt able to do with a complete stranger. Which was just as well, as I didn't realise how upset I was until I went away.

It's been said that the first full day away is when the wives get most thrown by the whole experience. Did you find that happened with you?

Yes, it really hits you then. But I got more unhappy as the filming went on. In fact, after the third day they couldn't film me, I wouldn't let them, as I was just so upset. I'd be watching Dave, seeing how hard he worked for his family, how he had to do everything – he was brilliant – and I'd see myself.

To a viewer, it seems strange that Dave and Jason are so different, despite being brothers...

Their father left them when Jason was about five or six, and Dave was already a teenager. As his Dad wasn't there, Jason's mother pampered him, trying to compensate for his father not being there, and this really just carried on as he grew up. When his mother went away for any reason, even when he was old enough to look after himself, she'd leave him a week's worth of dinners, she'd phone him to make sure he was up and out of bed when he had to go to work, and she'd even come round with a McDonald's breakfast to get him going in the morning. I had a very difficult relationship with her at first, but we get on very well now.

One of the strangest things about your episode is in the introduction when Jason says you do everything for money, that you have to be bribed. What was all that about?

I think that gives the wrong impression; it makes it look as if I was happy with that, when I wasn't. This whole thing about taking £20 for an errand or whatever came about because I would try to stand up to him, and tell him not to be lazy, to do something for himself. But when I realised he wouldn't, and that I'd have to do it anyway, then if he was silly enough to offer me money to do it for him, if he couldn't be persuaded to do it himself, I'd take his money.

I mean, it would be a case of him asking me to get him fish and chips at nine o'clock at night and he'd offer me £20 to go and get them. I'd say 'You're being ridiculous. £20 for fish and chips? You could get lobster for that…' It was a joke, not money-grabbing.

You obviously felt things like that and in fact, your whole life together, had to change. If he clearly hadn't come to the same conclusion when you met up at the reunion, would you really have left him?

Yes! At the end of the swap I really didn't want to go home, I was going to stay at a hotel and see a solicitor about our splitting up. That final day I was really nervous, butterflies in my stomach and all that. I didn't know what I was going to say to him. When we met I could tell that he was genuine about wanting to change and that he was upset too. He has changed, and has a better relationship with Lewis, who will want to show his Daddy something rather than show me. The trouble is he spends more time away now as his work takes him to Bath, but he does try when he's at home. He's definitely more loving towards them.

So it was a good experience for you, despite feeling so upset during the shoot?

It was very positive, but then I'd expected it to be in one sense. I'd entered us into the show, not really expecting to get on it, but about a week after I wrote in I got a phone call asking if we'd like to take part. I thought the whole thing would be a punishment for Jason. I hoped he'd get a really tough woman, a prison warden type, who'd make him realise how much I do. He used to accuse me of being a nag, but I don't nag him – I just wanted him to do something around the house and with the children. I don't think he realised just how much time he spent on his computer, and having someone else there would drum it into him. The trouble is he doesn't need much sleep, and he gets obsessive about the computer, and any new toys like that, and that was one on the main reasons for our rows and why I was often so close to walking out with the kids and leaving him. We were arguing all the time, and I thought the experience would be a good one for him. Which it was, because up until then he'd more or less had a bachelor's existence, with the benefit of a wife and kids when he wanted them. And now he's said 'I'm sorry, I'll change', and he means it.

And are you looking forward to watching your episode?

Yes we are, but it's also a bit worrying. I don't want to go into a shop or whatever and have someone say 'Oh, how could you live with that man?' Or, 'Shame about your husband, isn't it?' Even so, after the filming and when we got home we had a period of feeling really depressed, of thinking that perhaps we'd let too many home truths appear on television. We'll just have to see…

THE WIFE SWAP QUIZ, PART 4

How romantic is your partner?

1. His idea of demonstrating his love is...

a) daily surprises and reminders of how much he loves you.

b) occasional flowers and chocolates.

c) you have to buy your own anniversary card and if you're lucky he might sign it.

2. How often does he take you out to dinner?

a) At least every fortnight.

b) Two or three times a year, on special occasions.

c) He doesn't take you out to dinner, he sends you out for his favourite take-away.

3. His idea of sexy underwear is...

a) something slinky, sophisticated and extremely expensive from Agent Provocateur.

b) a Marks & Spencer three-pack of knickers.

c) his own pants hanging up in the bathroom.

4. His seduction technique involves...

a) dinner, fine wine and intimate conversation.

b) buying you a gin & tonic and cracking some bad jokes.

c) a grope.

KEY

Mostly A's: You are married to a perfect male specimen.

Mostly B's: At least you didn't have to pay for the gin & tonic.

Mostly C's: Did you know black widow spiders kill their males after mating? Just a thought.

Series 2 Episode 2

WIFE SWAP

The Couples

Colin and Emma Spry live in a smart modern house in Devon, with their two children. They take three holidays a year and describe themselves as aspirational and ambitious, with a belief in hard work and getting on in life. Colin manages a nightclub and Emma has an office job, but their great dream is to set up and run their own restaurant. Colin does much of the housework and cooks most of the meals, apparently Emma hasn't been near the cooker for six months. Though she loves her children and enjoys their company, she describes herself as 'not a natural mother'. They both wonder what the swap will be like: Emma says Colin hopes his temporary wife will be glamourous, and a good conversationalist. The main worry is the unknown quantity to the experience; what will they find and will both couples get on?

Lizzie and Mark Bardsley have eight children. Mark worked for the council for 14 years, but was made redundant two years ago and hasn't worked since. Lizzie came from a family of ten, so is used to

having a lot of people in the house. Her main concern is not so much what she will find at the other end, but whether the woman who is coming into her house can be trusted with her man. 'Will she be a trollop? Does she get a bit frisky after a drink?' Five of Lizzie's children are under four and even though she's used to children, she thinks any mother with several infants would agree that they can be exhausting to deal with at times. She hopes the new wife will be able to cope; if she can't, it'll be a 'nightmare' for her.

Arriving

The two wives arrive at their new homes and have a chance to look around. Lizzie thinks the Sprys' house is 'very posh', noticing 'she shops at Sainsburys!' She finds plenty of wine in the fridge, which is a good sign, 'I wonder how many of these I can drink in the next ten days?' she laughs. Compared to her large family, having only two or three children in the house will be a holiday! She's very surprised to read that Colin seems to do most of the housework, but less than impressed with them writing about how they don't like people without

the same sort of aspirations and drive as they have, 'we believe in hard work and do not like people who don't have ambitions.' Lizzie thinks it's insulting to write something like that in a Household Manual as it's almost designed to make the new wife feel unwelcome. That doesn't bode well...

In the Bardsley home, Emma is shocked to find there are eight children in the house. In fact, she has a quick cry at the idea as it seems overwhelming. She gets another shock when, reading the Household Manual, she discovers that the Bardsleys receive £37,000 after tax from the State in the form of various benefits. This is considerably more than she and Colin take home between them from their full time jobs. Is this a contrast too far?

Meet The Family

When the families meet, first impressions are mixed. Lizzie says to the Spry children 'Don't scream, but I've got eight children!' At the Bardsleys', Emma avoids crying, let alone screaming, but clearly the

mass of children is rather daunting. As soon as she meets Mark she says that she doesn't cook, so he and the kids shouldn't expect anything too exciting at dinner time.

Colin seems prepared to like Lizzie, 'She's very bubbly, a real Northern lass. I just hope we'll get on fine together!' Lizzie, on the other hand, is far from impressed with her new husband,

> *He's a wuss! He's all man and no balls, and a man with no balls is no good.*

Mark has a similarly robust view of Emma; 'It's really good to enjoy a meal that someone has made for you, so it was a real pisser when I found out she doesn't do much cooking.' Emma's view of the Bardsley household is simple,

Chaos!
It's absolute chaos.

Name: Lizzie Bardsley
Age: 29   Status: Married
Occupation: Unemployed
Location: Rochdale
Children: Elliot (12), Casey (11), Melody (8),
Marky Jay (4), Vienna (3), Saffron (2),
Anneka & Anouschka (1)

Getting To Know You...

As Emma works in an office, Lizzie agrees to try her hand at Emma's job – a daunting task as she hasn't worked for over ten years. Most of her work is fairly routine, including shredding documents. At the office she makes it clear that she thinks motherhood – especially of a large family – is harder work than going to an office: 'At the end of the day she can walk away. The kids are there 24 hours a day'. She thinks the office work is easy, and with only two children to pick up from school she finds that a doddle, too.

Emma is finding things far from easy with Mark. She feels he doesn't give her a lot of help, and that there is an overwhelming amount of housework to do. She thinks Mark is 'very arrogant' while he sees her as over-delicate: 'I think she's got a bit stressed, and when she arrived here I thought she was ready for cracking.' He doesn't think much of Emma's organisational skills, and grumbles,

Emma doesn't ever finish one job, she just moves on to something else before it's done.

Far from relaxing and letting Colin get on with all the domestic work, Lizzie is itching to get stuck in. Colin finds this irritating rather than helpful, as he has his own way of doing things, and isn't used to someone else offering an opinion on them. As a result Lizzie starts to wage a sort of guerrilla war against him, criticising what she sees as an extravagant and unnecessary lifestyle: 'Organic food? It tastes the same but costs twice as much!' According to her, Colin 'has got very set ideas about how to do things' and she finds him unable to even think about doing them differently. Colin thinks the same of Lizzie...

She's got so much to say... her trouble is she's too busy asking questions and isn't prepared to listen to the answer.

At the Bardsleys', Lizzie's mother comes round and starts suggesting that Lizzie actually does less than the Manual, and Mark, would have Emma believe. 'I've never seen Elizabeth with an iron in her hand,' she laughs. Emma, who is feeling exhausted by the sheer volume of work involved in coping with a house containing eight children, grasps the opportunity to reduce her workload to more

Mum, or Full-Time Entertainments Manager. Which one are you?

manageable levels, and confronts Mark on the issue. Mark gets very defensive but nevertheless Emma presses her point home. Isn't it true that Lizzie doesn't do any ironing? Why was that part of the Household Manual left blank? Emma suggests they throw the manual away as far as allocating duties is concerned, telling him 'that manual is full of lies!' Mark refuses to back down, and though he describes himself as a 'man of the twenty-first century', he won't accept Emma's argument that the reason the manual suggests his wife does so much is that he is embarrassed to admit how much work he actually does around the house.

Lizzie's problem is very different. Perhaps partly because she has so little to do around the house, she begins to brood on her nightmare scenario – that something might be going on between her husband and his stand-in wife. This fear erupts when Colin, hoping to cheer her up, takes her out for the sort of quiet romantic meal that he and Emma regularly enjoy.

Lizzie dolls herself up with her favourite hair-piece, exclaiming 'Instant long hair! Makes you feel a million dollars!' The trouble is she

When the green eyed monster rears its head in your household, how do you react?

thinks Emma might look a million dollars too, as she confides to Colin, 'another woman in your house is a threat'. Colin tries to put her at her ease, saying how much he trusts Emma, that she isn't that sort of woman, and that in any case, surely Lizzie trusts Mark? 'Trust in a relationship should be there', says Lizzie, 'but trust doesn't really come into it. You don't know what's going to happen, do you? You're not there to control the situation.' Colin stumbles on Lizzie's weak spot when he asks her how she feels about having an attractive blonde like his wife staying in her house while she's away. And when Lizzie lashes out about not knowing what another woman might get up to with her man, Colin concludes,

I do believe that out of the two of us, Emma and I have the strongest relationship.

Lizzie says she realises that Colin thinks she's arrogant and picky and that he doesn't like her, but that, 'Life's a bitch,' and on that note, she's going outside 'to partake of some nicotine'. Once in the cooler and calmer air outside the restaurant, she seems to calm down:

'I think I've got a lot off my chest.' She knows she's very different from Emma, but she obviously has a low opinion of her potential rival who she describes as 'a precious little Barbie doll.' Miaow!

Emma may be Barbie, but back at the Bardsleys', blondie is biting back. She won't give in on the housework issue, though Mark isn't conceding anything either. As far as he's concerned, her comments are just an excuse for her to do less work and he tells her, 'I think you should be pulling your weight a bit more.' When an increasingly frustrated Emma argues back, he just says, 'Some people are used to kids and others aren't.' Emma is worried about how she'll get through the next days and says miserably, 'I can't live in this house.' It's all going downhill and fast, but is the rollercoaster ride about to come to a sudden end?

As it's the twins' first birthday, the usual *Wife Swap* rules are bent a little, so that Lizzie can phone home. When she does so, Emma is feeling very emotional – something Lizzie has no sympathy for. She still sees her as a threat, and asks Mark for reassurance, 'So you don't fancy her then? Are you sure? She doesn't do anything for you?'

Going on a date can reinvigorate your relationship, so get your hair-piece on and dress up for a night out without the kids once in a while!

Mark takes the call on his portable phone, and follows the tearful Emma into the kitchen. Speaking to Lizzie and within earshot of Emma, he tells his wife that, 'She's stood at the back door, crying.' 'Life's a bitch!' snaps back Lizzie. Mark says he doesn't think Emma will last the full ten days, 'I don't reckon she'll make it,' and Lizzie blames this on what she sees as Emma's laziness: if she'd been used to doing more work at home, like a normal housewife, she wouldn't be finding the work involved in running the Bardsleys' house so difficult. Hmm...

The next day it's clear that her conversation with Mark has had quite the opposite of its desired effect. Far from reassuring Lizzie, it has led to her having a sleepless night and her fretting has brought on her asthma. She isn't up to going to work, and can't face the housework either. Colin's efforts to get her to do anything are ignored, as she wallows in her misery, 'She's got everything and I've got nothing. That's the way it feels.'

At the Bardsleys', Emma has, by contrast, had a great night's sleep, and she seems a lot more confident. She and Mark also seem to be getting on better, and Emma cooks her first major meal. The result goes down very well, and Mark is delighted: 'Ten out of ten for effort,' and comments that when she gets home Colin could be redundant in the kitchen. Colin has other things on his mind. Tip-toeing around the house, he concludes,

> *I just think she's jealous that a beautiful woman has gone into her home.*

This proves to be exactly the case, and Lizzie decides to call an abrupt halt the swap. She moves into a local hotel and phones Mark, telling him to get rid of Emma immediately. Mark tries to talk to her but she won't budge – he thinks she's 'totally off her head!' Matters aren't improved when Mark tells Emma that she's got to pack her bags and leave. Emma asks why and Lizzie tells her, via Mark, to mind her own business – it's Lizzie's house, not hers. She accuses Emma of being lazy, of not having looked after the babies properly. Emma laughs, which winds Lizzie up even more. Go, girl!

Ladies, do you believe there is such a creature as a Twenty-First Century Man? Or is he a myth?!

Mark tells the camera that the real reason for Lizzie's decision appears to be that she has found out, in conversation with Colin, that he had been married when he met Emma. As far as Lizzie is concerned, this is a 'red alarm bell'. Emma is a marriage wrecker. Once a wrecker – however long ago – always a wrecker, and she isn't going to have such a woman in her house for another moment. That's the end of that, then.

Taking Stock

The families, despite this dramatic early end to the experiment, do agree to meet up for the traditional post-swap reunion. The reunion sees even more sparks flying than usual, and most of them are coming from Lizzie, whose comments are delivered at an impressive volume. Things get off to a bad start when Mark says he thinks the Sprys look down on him and Lizzie as 'spongers'. Colin and Emma agree, and Emma says she thinks he should get a job and have his independence. She also thinks that smoking in a house full of children is a bad idea – something that immediately brings a sarcastic response from Lizzie who cries, 'Dr Emma in the house!' Her animosity towards Emma is unrelenting, 'Your whole life is a farce… You're Miss Penelope…' Emma says 'You seem fascinated by me', which irritates Lizzie even more, giving rise to an outburst of,

Don't sit there fluttering your eyelids at my husband!

When Emma defends herself she gets an even angrier retort of 'You snooty f***ing cow!' Calm down, calm down.

Emma defuses things somewhat when describing how she had fallen for Colin when she was very young, and that though she knows what she did was wrong she was blinded by love. This provokes a tender response from Lizzie, who talks movingly of how much she loves her husband and children. She understands now that when you leave them for a while, 'You realise you love them even more, they are the most precious thing to you…' and it's a relief to see the softer side to her by the end of the show.

The View From The Sofa

The Sprys start the programme at a disadvantage as they appear to be very pleased with themselves and with what they have achieved together. They seem to look down on anyone who doesn't share their lifestyle; something they even put in the Household Manual. But as the swap goes on, Emma comes across well, and Colin is at least trying to be nice the whole time. Lizzie, who is clearly a great mother, is like the proverbial fish out of water when she is away from her family, and she's so stressed at the idea of an attractive woman staying in her home, it's surprising she went in for the swap in the first place. Presumably she didn't realise quite how strongly she'd feel until she was actually away from home and the phone call seemed counter-productive, because although it made her feel much happier about things in the short term, it obviously gave her a lot to think about. Her decision to call the whole thing off showed that the programme wasn't so much about the difference between a small family and a large one. Neither was it about the social division between an ambitious couple and a couple on long-term state benefits; instead, it was about the issue of personal jealousy.

At the reunion in particular, Lizzie came across as being very loud and argumentative, combining a refusal to listen to anyone with an aggression and contempt for Colin and Emma. Mark did his best to get a word in but gave up the unequal struggle. Emma's calm reaction to Lizzie's rage initially seemed to infuriate her all the more, and it was only when Emma spoke of her love for Colin that there seemed to be any sort of fellow-feeling between the two women. Certainly, this was one of the more interesting shows, with the green-eyed monster rearing its head between the two wives for the first time, but maybe not the last…

THE WIFE SWAP QUIZ, PART 5

How good a housekeeper are you?

1. The best way to clean a wooden floor is to...

a) sweep it first then get on your hands and knees and give it a good polish with floor wax.

b) run around with a mop every now and again.

c) carpet over it.

2. How often do you clean your windows?

a) Once a month, inside and out.

b) As often as the window cleaner comes round to do it for me.

c) Hey, having dirty windows saves money on curtains.

3. How often do you do the household food shopping?

a) Every day at a farmers' market to make sure you have the freshest produce.

b) Every week at the out-of-town supermarket.

c) Every day at McDonalds.

4. Regular laundry is...

a) important for a clean and healthy lifestyle.

b) a necessary evil.

c) for wimps.

KEY

Mostly A's: Congratulations, you are qualified to run a stately home.

Mostly B's: Sometimes just knowing how to use the Hoover can be enough.

Mostly C's: There's a fine line between lady of leisure and bag-lady of leisure.

Series 2 Episode 3

WIFE SWAP

The Couples

Kellie and Raff have been together for two years. Kellie has three children, is a teacher and has survived breast cancer. Her fitness regime, inspired and driven by her earlier fight with the disease, means that she eats only organic (vegetarian) food. She insists that her family follow her diet, and won't have meat or dairy products in the house. In their home the domestic chores are divided among the entire family, with the children playing their part as well as Raff. He describes her as 'bossy' and says that if she wants him to do something 'she will stay on my back until it's done.'

Justin and Maxine have been together for seven years. She has two daughters and they have a son, aged two. Maxine works as a cleaner for four hours a day, beginning work at 5.30am. She is also a full-time housewife who does the domestic chores. Justin, who works as a timber salesman, is proud of the fact that when at home he likes 'to play, not graft' and that when it comes to helping around the house he's 'barely lifted a finger' during the whole time he has been with Maxine.

Name: Raphael Gibson
Age: **46**
Occupation: **Care Worker in Children's Home**

As a family they don't go in for organic food, nor are they big on fruit and veg – Justin doesn't like carrots or greens, the only vegetables that he'll eat are potatoes and peas. The family have a history of rows, apparently 'we bitch big time.' You could make a show just on their different diets alone, so how will each react to these new taste sensations?

Arriving

As always both wives get the chance to look around their temporary homes before their new families arrive. Kellie's first question as she looks around the kitchen, exploring the fridge and the cupboards, is 'Any fruit and veg?'. Maxine is amused to discover a 'nutrition bible': she wonders how Kellie will manage with Justin.

They read the Household Manuals that have been left for them, and Kellie realises that she's in for a bit of a struggle: Justin does not cook and Maxine does all the housework. This is completely different

Name: Kellie Ansell
Age: **41**   Status: **Partners**
Occupation: **Teacher**
Location: **Peckham**
Children: **Asher (16), Jessie (14), Joel (12)**

to the way she runs her own house. However, she's quite prepared to live by Maxine's rules for the first five days. What she's really looking forward to, though, is getting the chance to implement her own rules in the second half of the swap and expects to be able to open the new family's eyes to the benefits of organic food and lots of fruit.

Meet The Family

Kellie and Justin seem to get along all right to start with, though there's a real sense of this being the calm before the storm, as both of them are such strong – and different – characters. Kellie says that she thinks Justin is really hyper, with loads of energy, but he doesn't know how to concentrate… there are lots of alarm bells ringing. Maxine's daughters have really taken to her, and one says to camera, 'I give her ten out of ten. She's really fun. Brill! Wow!' Possibly one of the nicest first reactions in *Wife Swap* history, but how much will this change over the course of the ten days ahead?

Name: Justin Wells
Age: **30**
Occupation: **Timber Salesman**

Back at Kellie's house, Maxine is finding it hard to settle in. She's a quieter, less forceful (superficially, anyway) person than Kellie, and she's already homesick and misses her family, 'I really miss the kids. And Justin, even if he is a lazy git!' Raff is sympathetic, though disappointed at her failure to make much of an impact. He thinks that she'll gradually find her feet, saying hoping 'she'll become more relaxed'. This being a non-smoking household, Maxine's sense of isolation is emphasised by the fact that she has to stand, outside the house on her lonesome whenever she wants a cigarette. Uh-oh…

Getting To Know You…

Kellie finds getting up on her first morning at Maxine's house, after just four hours sleep, very hard. Although she puts her back into the cleaning job, it's clear from her comment 'this wouldn't be my career choice!' that it's not the sort of work she would ever have considered for herself. When she gets home from work she has a mass of housework to do, and she finds this depressing and dull, stating 'I feel like I'm penned in the house.'

Name: Maxine Bate
Age: **31** Status: **Partners**
Occupation: **Cleaner**
Location: **Battersea, London**
Children: **Antonella Bate (12), Amy Beasley (9)**
Dre Wells (2)

She continues to make a good impression on the girls, however, but they, in turn, are less than impressed with Justin's attempts to ingratiate himself with the newcomer: 'He's really trying to show off in front of her – and she's way out of his league!' Their taking to Kellie is at least partly influenced by the fact that they seem to have quite a tempestuous relationship with their stepfather and arguments between them are a regular occurrence.

Maxine takes on Kellie's job as a teacher at a nursery school. This is providing far more stimulus for her and she's also very good with children. She likes the children she's looking after at home, but has her reservations, on several levels, about how they've been brought up. She thinks that they and Raff help around the house too much, but on the other hand she thinks the younger two children aren't in the house enough. They both seem to be falling into a street culture – their older sister refers to them as 'street rats' – and she thinks the time they spend just wandering about outside is dangerous for them. She would much rather she knew where they were and what they were doing.

Cut back on the additives for a less hyper husband!

Roles within a family are one of the discussion points when Justin takes Kellie and the children to his mother's for a family visit. This is preceded by a row with the older of his stepdaughters. Kellie sides with the girl, who is very upset that Justin has said she doesn't do anything, when she has spent the day trying to be helpful. Kellie tries to persuade him to apologise to her, on the grounds that not only has she actually been helpful, and that Justin is therefore in the wrong – or, at the least, very tactless – but unless he does calm her down, the family outing will be ruined. Kellie doesn't expect Justin to apologise (that would certainly be a bridge too far) but can't he at least tell her that he appreciates what she's done today? After all, she only wants a little recognition.

When peace breaks out and they actually make it over to Justin's mother's, Kellie realises where he gets a lot of his attitude towards male/female relationships from: his mother has very traditional views of the respective roles of the sexes: 'Justin does what a man's supposed to do, and Maxine does what a woman's supposed to do.' Kellie grins and bears it, especially when her comments about bringing up her son to be a modern man, who will therefore go into a marriage as an equal, seem to fall on deaf ears.

Turning The Tables

Maxine and Kellie both look forward to turning their new households upside down, though in Kellie's case it's out-and-out war, whereas Maxine has settled into her new household and is more relaxed. She's also happier with her new family than Kellie, so her changes, though radical, aren't influenced by a desire for revenge or the sort of missionary zeal to spread the word about a better way of life that Kellie is so keen on.

Kellie tells the camera that rather than gradually introduce changes (which would involve the sort of diplomatic approach that she was earlier urging Justin to use towards his stepdaughter) she has decided 'to go for the hard knock'. Justin will have to pull his weight and help look after the children, whether he likes it or not. Echoing Lizzie Bardsley's catchphrase, she says,

Life's a bitch – get over it.

It's easy to make such a statement when talking to yourself in front of a camera that doesn't answer back. But what will it be like when she has Justin standing there in front of her?

The moment comes for her to sit the family down and break them the news: chips will be served only once a week. The rest of the time they'll have to follow her healthy diet, like it or not! Justin is told he's not to swear in front of the children, and nor is he to call them names. This doesn't go down well, as it's clear that cleaning up his language isn't going to be high on his list of priorities when he says, of life's problems (including Kellie's rules)

If I can't handle it, my main word is 'bollocks'.

Fair enough.

It doesn't have to be chips with everything – go crazy and get some salad in your diet!

'Bollocks' – and worse – are soon flying around the kitchen when Justin finds that not only has Kellie changed the food, but she's also taken away his, and the children's, fizzy drinks. When he realises that she's also changed two year old Dre's drink, he goes ballistic. Kellie stands her ground, arguing that very young children need all the help they can get when it comes to nutrition and that at that age they'll more or less take what they're given. So, is Justin's outburst to do with having the little 'un's best interests at heart, or is it just about what he wants, we wonder? As Kellie is going out for the evening, she leaves Justin to cook the family meal, using her ingredients. He plays by the rules in cooking it, but rushes into the kitchen to spit it out, something he makes a real meal out of. Anyone would think she'd actually made him eat bollocks rather than just driven him to shouting it!

Maxine's changes, though gentler than Kellie's, are still radical. She is, by now, getting on better with the family, and although Kellie's son is frustrated at being told to spend less time on the street, the family don't fight back. To add insult to injury, Maxine threatens to walk along with him when he goes out, so she knows where he is; blimey, can you imagine the loss of street cred?

In fact, when Maxine and Raff join forces for a family barbecue, complete with the sort of traditional food like sausages, bacon and hamburgers that Kellie won't allow in the house, they all get on tremendously and have a great time; aah, there's nothing like a family bonding over a nicely cooked banger! Maxine's belief that they need to do more as a family unit together is something they've very happily taken on board and are enjoying doing and Raff tells her that even once she's gone home, he and the children will probably want to carry on having the occasional barbeque. The two of them seem to have cemented their friendship over the burnt sausages:

Me and you were total strangers, and at least through this I've met a new friend.

Friendship, however, seems to be the last thing on the agenda at the Wells/Bate house. In fact, Justin has bought the children a McDonalds take-away in an act of rebellion. Kellie is furious and corners him in the kitchen: 'I've done everything your way for five days, now you're supposed to keep my rules. Proper nutrition is very important, it plays an important part in keeping people healthy, keeping their skin good, avoiding illness...' She sees she may as well be talking to the wall, as Justin is sitting with his back towards her, sulking, but also pleased with himself over this act of defiance. Unable to crack this stubborn rebellion, Kellie pities what Maxine must go through every day as a matter of course. It seems there will be a lot to talk about at the reunion, especially as Kellie appears to have hit a nerve, because Justin is desperately missing Maxine, and we see him, on several occasions, clinging to their two year old son, while looking utterly miserable. Talking to the camera, he admits how upset he is at Maxine not being there, 'I can't handle it. It's too much... I feel like I've been kicked in the teeth.'

Returning the favour of the bonding-bbq, Raff takes Maxine on a day trip away from the house to Brighton. As he says, it took a couple of days for them to 'suss each other out', but they get on fine. In fact, they agree that in many ways they are like each other, especially in that each of them has a very dominant partner who they think takes them for granted. Raff in particular thinks he needs to change things when Kellie gets back.

I need to be more assertive, and she needs to learn that 'no' means no!

Kellie is looking forward to going home, especially as she has had a major row with Justin over the fact that, under her rules, he should be helping out a lot around the house. Justin argues that after having done a day's work, he deserves some help from Kellie in putting Amy to bed. 'I've been doing the washing, the cooking, the cleaning and looking after the children and I deserve to get some help here…' I think we've seen this kind of reaction when the tables are turned on the *Wife Swap* men-folk before, haven't we?! Kellie is less than impressed at this, and doesn't hold back on sharing her thoughts to the video diary.

He's ignorant, he's rude, and he has no self-control. Maxine must be either a martyr or a saint. I'm going to tell it like it is, and sort this man out!

Justin, however, decides he's had enough and from now on will ignore Kellie's rules, because 'I'm the boss in my own house.' Faced with a complete breakdown in their relationship, Kellie manages a magnificent level of understatement when she says 'This has not been a very nice experience!' Justin is more emphatic, especially over a row about food, when he says that even if his food is 'shit' in nutritional terms, it is what he is used to, and is what he is going to eat, whether she likes it or not. 'I love shit, I eat shit, I'm built of shit!' There's just no answer to that…

In a striking contrast to the Justin/Kellie scenario, Maxine decides to take her temporary family for an outing and treats them to a night at the dog races. Everyone has a great time, and we see how it is possible for very different people to get on, when they all try to make a go of it. What will both sets of couples make of their experience when they actually meet face to face, before going back to their homes?

Taking Stock

The reunion, predictably, sees Justin and Kellie doing most of the talking, but Raff pipes up as well, much to Kellie's surprise, and although Justin has been rather, er, 'difficult' during the programme, at the reunion he becomes surprisingly calm and persuasive, and takes Kellie completely by surprise with his new attitude.

Kellie starts by saying how she finds Justin 'really rude' and hates how he speaks to her. Justin agrees with her, but argues that, in a way, this isn't really his fault as 'I don't realise what I'm saying, half the time.' Maxine says she doesn't want another argument but that she realises she needs to be appreciated more at home, something Raff also agrees with in his relationship with Kellie.

Justin then shocks Kellie by saying that he and she are actually alike:

We're built from the same frame. At home your rules are arranged around you and what you like... everyone does things for us.

Justin claims that he has always, as he puts it 'had my arse wiped for me'. Fortunately he doesn't use the same image when referring to Kellie, but he does say to her, when she strongly denies that he and she have anything in common at all, 'You like to be in control. In fact I've learnt a lot from you. You try and control the shop...'

When Raff tries to stand up for himself about how things are run at his house, opening with, 'Maxine's life and mine are quite similar...' Kellie slaps him down, especially when he says he wants to be appreciated more for what he does around the house. Doesn't she do a lot? Why shouldn't she be appreciated then? What's he on about? 'Just because you're a man, why can't you thank me for what I do?' Here we go again...

Gallantly, Justin does actually thank Maxine for what she does for the family, saying

From this experience I've learned to appreciate Maxine

and after the reunion is over and the couples return home, we learn that Justin has indeed turned over a new leaf and has booked himself a place on an anger management course. Kellie, on getting home, is horrified at what has been put in her fridge, finds some milk, and despite Raff's plea that he could use it in his coffee, she grimly pours it down the kitchen sink. She's back, and she's in charge. The End.

The View From The Sofa

Until the reunion, it's hard to like Justin very much. He seems totally hyper (though his little dance when the family go to visit his mum is funny) and he also seems totally resistant to change. His antics when cooking the organic meal that Kellie has instructed him to make seem pretty petty, in contrast to Kellie's very calm, rational and reasonable demeanour. The strain she is under from living in the same house as Justin – and which she refers to at the reunion – is clearly shown in the course of the programme, especially in the video diaries. By the end of the show she looks completely knackered!

Yet at the reunion Justin showed exactly the sort of self-knowledge and ability to rationalise a situation that is supposed to be an essential ingredient of *Wife Swap* candidates, but which until that moment (as far as we could tell via the camera, at any rate) he hadn't shown. Kellie seemed as taken by surprise as the viewer on the sofa at his about-face, and wasn't as effective in defending herself as we might have expected. In the end, Justin seemed to win his particular point – that he and she were both strong, controlling people, and that though she might be a lot quieter than him and seemingly his opposite in many ways, she was actually as insistent on getting her own way as he was.

These last five minutes redressed the balance in the programme, and saw Raff, a mild mannered man, also make a stand, even if he could only watch helplessly as Kellie poured the milk that Maxine had brought into the house down the sink. There's no doubt about it, this swap this was very good value, with Maxine's quietly effective revolution – family days out were good, there was more than one choice of food in the world, Kellie wasn't perfect – as constructive and in its own way as interesting as the more conventionally exciting battle of wills between Justin and Kellie.

THE WIFE SWAP QUIZ, PART 6

How laid back a parent are you?

1. The kids have run riot, leaving the house in a state of chaos. Do you...

a) not mind, or even notice, for that matter?

b) gather them together and calmly insist they tidy up after themselves immediately?

c) scream, collapse and bang your head against the floor repeatedly?

2. You're supposed to be picking up one of your kids, but she is five minutes late. What do you do?

a) Not even realise she's late.

b) Roll your eyes and turn on the radio.

c) Panic, phone home to see if there's any word of her movements, then sit, glaring like a maniac when she does at last turn up.

3. Your child has just insulted someone to their face. Do you...

a) secretly agree with them?

b) Quietly correct her and make them apologise to the person concerned?

c) barrel into their room and scream that they're 'a rude, arrogant, nasty cesspit of a child'?

4. What's the worst thing you've ever let your husband get away with?

a) Most things, actually.

b) Taking you for granted and not doing his share of the work.

c) Buying blue toilet roll when your bathroom colour scheme clearly dictates that only WHITE or CREAM will do!

KEY

Mostly A's: You are so laid back that you're not even vertical any more. Be careful not to fall over.

Mostly B's: Congratulations. The essential oils and candles in the bath are clearly doing the trick.

Mostly C's: You are a ticking time bomb of unexpressed rage. You might want to take up yoga. (And put down the knife.)

WIFE SWAP

This book was going to press when episode four of the second series of *Wife Swap* was being edited, so we spoke to its director, Simon Davies, to see what he could tell us about his show.

What can you tell us about the programme? What was your intention behind choosing the two couples involved, and what issues arose from it?

My episode features the Collinsons from Bognor Regis, who run a guest house, and the Lavins from Liverpool, who run a pub.

What I really wanted to examine is what it is like to be a woman in contemporary society, where she is often expected to be a wife and mother as well as someone who goes out to work. It's a contemporary dilemma that many women face, and the question that goes with it is, do men really support their wives? And the answer is, no!

Can you tell us about each couple in turn? What are they like? How does their family work?

The Collinson family run a very picturesque guest house, The Old Priory, in Bognor Regis. It's a sixteenth-century priory with a swimming pool and a jacuzzi; it's very attractive. Deborah and Nigel have been married for 24 years and they have two teenage sons. Nigel also runs a couple of computer shops, and between them they have a good income.

The dynamic in their relationship is that he offers her support in a superficial way, financial and business fronts, but he completely undermines her decisions in the household. He never backs her up and he's always finding excuses for the kids if she has a problem with them.

The boys treat the place, to use the phrase, as a hotel. As far as they're concerned it's a sort of social club, and their friends are always round there, as are their girlfriends, Nicky and Leanne. This causes problems for Deborah because, the Priory's guests

sometimes complain about the noisy music, the parties, the towels and beer bottles left round the swimming pool…

The Lavin family consists of Steve, Linda and their children Jessica, and Mitchell. Linda is a pub landlady and has a flat above the pub that goes with the job. The pub, in Liverpool, is an Everton supporters' pub, though Steve is a Liverpool fan.

Linda has to get up at about 7am to get the kids ready, take them to school, and then is down in the pub from 9am supervising the cleaners. She runs the pub until 4pm, when she has a break, but the time between 4pm and 9pm is, in effect, spent running the flat and getting the children's dinner and putting them to bed.

Steve's background is that he could have been a professional footballer but had a knee injury, so now plays in a semi-professional capacity as a goalkeeper. His main interests other than football are darts and drinking. Every Friday at 4pm Linda gives him £50 'pocket money' to spend on what he wants. Linda is more like his mother than his wife, in that she does everything for him.

Name: **Stephen Lavin**
Age: **41**
Occupation: **Unemployed**

Why do you think these couples wanted to take part in *Wife Swap*?

Basically, because it gave them a chance to step out from their lives, to see how other people do things and with a view to assessing their own lives in the light of this experience.

So, how did they find the experience?

When Linda arrived at Bognor Regis she thought 'Great! It's beautiful... I won't want to go home!' But almost immediately she realised what the problem was, that the boys didn't treat it like the family home and that they made no contribution to the household. There was a major issue of respect, which I found fascinating, because Linda comes from a very strong working class tradition where you respect your parents; for example, she still won't smoke in front of her mother. She found a lot of what went on at the Collinsons' very disturbing – including the fact that their girlfriends stayed over, that there were posters about dope around, and that Nigel was such a fudger when it came to any sort of discipline.

Name: Linda Lavin
Age: 34 Status: Married
Occupation: Pub Landlady
Location: Liverpool
Children: Jessica (9), Mitchell (2)

On her first full day she asked him, 'What are the guidelines? At what point do we stop a party?' The noise of one of their parties caused a complaint from the neighbours, there was a row with Aaron, and she turned the music off herself, as Nigel was no real help at all.

What did she do to change things?

When it was time for her to impose her rules, she said Aaron had to be home by 11pm, that the girlfriends couldn't stay the night and that he had to cook two breakfasts a week and a dinner.

What are the boys like?

Aaron is good looking in a sort of boy-band way, plays the guitar, is liked by girls… Karl is a bit older and more settled, more of a homebody. Their relationship with Deborah reminds me of that television series, *Butterflies*, with Wendy Craig, even though Deborah is also a bit like Sybil from *Fawlty Towers*. Aaron walked out after Linda set her rules, but he came back, although he was never in before 11pm and he only cooked one breakfast.

Linda set the curfew at 11pm but Nigel would approach Aaron and say 'Well, let's say 11.30' as a sort of compromise, but actually undermining her completely. He comes across as a weak man, frightened of confrontation. He didn't like Linda's approach at all, and said that he'd distance himself from her, that he'd be polite but that as far as he was concerned she wasn't a temporary member of the family, she was 'just a guest.'

What happened in Liverpool?

Deborah was appalled at the Household Manual she read, and within two minutes she'd nailed Steve, saying 'I'm really worried about him. He doesn't support her at all, he does nothing, he doesn't help with the children…' It was quite funny really, as Steve couldn't even sit down before she laid into him. She gave him a grilling for about an hour, and he went silent, then just walked away at the end of it.

As Deborah realised, Linda does everything, Steve does nothing. When he gets hammered of an evening his father puts him to bed! It's a close-knit community and everyone lives near each other. Steve had his first ever pint at that pub, his dad drinks there. and he knows, all the regulars. As Linda says, there's one dickhead in every pub, and she finds it mortifying that the one in her pub is her husband!

He must have some redeeming qualities, though?

He gets very affectionate when he's plastered. Naturally, the drinking was something Deborah picked up on and when it came to her turn to set the household rules she insisted that he go without a drink for the five days during which he had to live her way. He also had to get up early to help with the kids, to have a family day out, and to look for work. He also had to walk the dog. Their dog is a character in its own right, a Highland terrier called Chloe.

Did he keep to the 'no drink' rule?

He played in a disastrous football match in which he let in ten goals, so he claimed he needed a drink to cope with the depression. But if his side had won the match, that would have been given as an equally valid reason why he should break the rule and have a drink, too.

Deborah tried to cut down on the drink by only giving him £20 pocket money instead of £50, but his friends lent him some money so he got hammered anyway!

What did the wives make of the experience?

I think the programme was unique in that instead of having a go at each other during the reunion meeting, they actually got on very well and were supportive of each other. This was wonderful, because in previous programmes the women seemed to be really threatened by each other. Linda and Deborah wanted to know how each coped with the other's problems. Both Nigel and Steve had to listen to some basic home truths as the two women discussed them.

It's only been four or so weeks since we shot the film but the women are trying to make their families abide by some of the changes that the other woman tried to introduce. Steve is more helpful around the house – Linda told me he made her a cup of tea the other day – and they had a long weekend away in Bournemouth, so perhaps the swap has helped her to make some changes.

5 REASONS WHY YOU SHOULD COUNT YOUR BLESSINGS...

1. Your kids may be swearing near you, but they're not swearing at you.

2. Where would you put a second car anyway?

3. Your kids may not be getting straight A's at school, but at least they're not giant swots.

4. Your husband may not be an Adonis, but at least it means the girls at his workplace won't be tempted.

5. Well, if your life was perfect, everyone else would hate you anyway.

5 *REASONS WHY*
THE GRASS IS GREENER ON THE OTHER SIDE...

1. You think your friends' children are so angelic? Just add sugar.

2. Your neighbour's house is only that tidy because they know when you're coming round.

3. He may look good, but he's probably rubbish in bed.

4. A house that big costs a fortune to heat anyway.

5. Money can't buy you taste – just look at Elton John.

Swapping Continents

The Brits may not rule the waves any more, but they still make great television, as *Wife Swap* has proved. Broadcasters have now taken up the series, which was an immediate hit for Channel 4, across the world. For those who like the background info, there are three ways of promoting a television series overseas: selling the series as it is, which usually applies to English-speaking territories like the United States, Canada, New Zealand and Australia; selling the concept (where foreign companies make local language versions) and making it locally yourself, as is sometimes the case in the United States.

Wife Swap's genius lies in the fact that the format could be applied to pretty much any country or culture in the world. Not only that it has a huge potential for cross-cultural programming and there's already talk of an Anglo-American wife swap across the Atlantic. In the global village that commentators now tell us the world has become, the possibilities of experiencing a genuinely different way of life, in a foreign landscape, is far more easily affordable and achievable now than at any time in the past, especially if the recent trend for 'reality/lifestyle' television shows which follow the progress of UK citizens who move overseas to start new lives is anything to go by.

An international *Wife Swap* raises more questions about how the show would translate. For example, if the series is about relationships rather than race or class, then how strongly would the influence of national/cultural identity be felt? Wouldn't it be more likely that the potential for conflict, confusion and misunderstanding would be even greater when contrasting nationalities are thrown into the mix? It's an interesting concept and one that would certainly be great to watch!

International intentions aside, it's been a refreshing experience in viewing *Wife Swap* to feel like rather more than just a bystander in such a popular and rewarding show. Despite the brickbats thrown by some commentators who simply dislike reality TV and/or refuse to see the difference between the programmes that can loosely fall into that category, *Wife Swap* has genuinely improved the lives of those who have taken part, not in terms of financial reward but in terms of insight, happiness and more successful relationships.

It is a particularly enjoyable irony, in an age of self-help manuals and therapy sessions that the best way of finding yourself remains through experiencing other people. *Wife Swap* has achieved this in its United Kingdom format and looks set to spread the message – and the results – on television screens across the world. The possibilities really are endless…